Study Guide
for the
U.S. Adult Catholic Catechism

Jem Sullivan, Ph.D.

Our Sunday Visitor Publishing Division

Our Sunday Visitor, Inc.

Huntington, IN 46750

Nihil Obstat: Rev. Michael Heintz, Ph.D., *Censor Librorum*
Imprimatur: ✠John M. D'Arcy
Bishop of Fort Wayne-South Bend
August 15, 2006

The *Nihil Obstat* and *Imprimatur* are official declarations that a book or pamphlet is free of doctrinal or moral error. No implication is contained therein that those who have granted the *Nihil Obstat* or *Imprimatur* agree with the contents, opinions, or statements expressed.

The Scripture citations used in this work are taken from the *Catholic Edition of the Revised Standard Version of the Bible* (RSV), copyright © 1965 and 1966 by the Division of Christian Education of the National Council of the Churches of Christ in the United States of America. Used by permission. All rights reserved.

Catechism excerpts are from the English translation of the *Catechism of the Catholic Church, Second Edition,* for use in the United States of America, copyright © 1994 and 1997, United States Catholic Conference — Libreria Editrice Vaticana. Used by permission. All rights reserved.

English translations of *Gaudium et Spes, Dei Verbum, Lumen Gentium,* and *Ad Gentes* from the Vatican website, www.vatican.va.

Every reasonable effort has been made to determine copyright holders of excerpted materials and to secure permissions as needed. If any copyrighted materials have been inadvertently used in this work without proper credit being given in one form or another, please notify Our Sunday Visitor in writing so that future printings of this work may be corrected accordingly.

Our Sunday Visitor Publishing Division
Our Sunday Visitor, Inc.
200 Noll Plaza
Huntington, IN 46750

ISBN: 978-1-59276-206-4 (Inventory No. X257)
LCCN: 2006933117

Cover design by Monica Haneline
Interior design by Laura Klynstra
Cover photo: *The Annunciation* (Fra Carnevale), Samuel H. Kress Collection. Image © 2006 Board of Trustees, National Gallery of Art, Washington, DC. Used with permission.

PRINTED IN THE UNITED STATES OF AMERICA

✦ INTRODUCTION ✦

"I wish I knew more about my faith so I could be a better witness to others," says a young mother who finds herself in debates with other parents.

"I would love to keep learning more about the basics of my newfound Catholic faith," notes a recent convert to Catholicism.

"I know I should read and reflect more on faith, but with all the information out there, I don't quite know where to begin!" admits a young college graduate.

How often have we heard it said that a renewal of catechesis is critically needed in our time? In the face of the many "isms" that plague our society — consumerism, materialism, secularism, relativism, to name a few — men, women, and children continue to seek to know, love, and live the Catholic faith in the midst of culture. Church renewal in our time goes hand-in-hand with a renewed catechesis aimed at conversion of life, holiness, and witness rooted in the beauty and fullness of the Church's teachings.

If you share in this desire to deepen knowledge of your Catholic faith and strengthen your witness of faith and love to others, this Study Guide to the *United States Catholic Catechism for Adults* is offered as a timely catechetical and faith formation resource.

History of the *United States Catholic Catechism for Adults*

When Pope John Paul II presented the *Catechism of the Catholic Church* to Catholics and to the world on December 7, 1992, he described it as a "sure and authentic reference point" that provides a synthesis of the fundamental content of Catholic doctrine, regarding faith and morals, in light of the Second Vatican Council and the Church's Tradition. The Universal Catechism is a gift of and to the

Church in our times as it offers a comprehensive and authoritative summary of the Catholic faith. Since its publication more than a decade ago, the Catechism has become an indispensable means of catechetical renewal as it invites a daily and lifelong conversion of the whole person — mind, body, and heart — to a "living, conscious and active faith."

In response to the need for a deeper appropriation of the riches of the Universal Catechism, a special commission established by Pope John Paul II prepared a Compendium, or "mini-Catechism," published in June 2005. In introducing this Compendium to the Church, Pope Benedict XVI notes that it "represents an additional resource for satisfying the hunger for truth among the Christian faithful of all ages and conditions, as well as the hunger for truth and justice among those who are without faith."

In recent years, the Catholic bishops of America have responded to the need for catechetical renewal in this country by preparing a *United States Catholic Catechism for Adults*. This national catechism relates the fundamental content of Church teaching to the concrete context of American culture. It draws on the teachings and structure of the Universal Catechism and reflects the unity of the Catholic faith in content and language, as well as the richness of its lived expression in America.

This Study Guide, or Companion, to the *United States Catholic Catechism for Adults* is offered as an accessible and practical catechetical tool to accompany use of the national catechism. Catholic adults in a variety of catechetical settings may use this Study Guide to gain deeper access to the profound riches of the Catechism's four pillars — the Creed, the Sacraments, Christian Life, and Prayer. A faithful reading and understanding of the new *United States Catholic Catechism* is now made readily accessible with this compact Study Guide.

What Is a National Catechism?

The *United States Catholic Catechism for Adults* is an adaptation of the Universal Catechism that follows the basic catechetical plan of the Catechism's "four pillars" in the Creed, the Sacraments, the Christian Life, and Prayer.

Written specifically for American Catholic adults, the national catechism presents the fullness and wealth of Church teaching within the American cultural context as it draws on examples of American saints and local witnesses to the faith.

The adult catechism follows in the tradition of local adaptations of the universal *Catechism of the Catholic Church* for Catholics of different cultures and languages throughout the world. It is a distinct expression of Catholic unity based on a common language of faith and Catholic identity, shaped by the particular cultural context in which that faith is lived. As a unique catechetical tool, it reflects the unity of the Catholic faith and the richness of its lived expression in American culture at the dawn of the third Christian millennium.

Why a National Catechism?

"All politics is local," quipped Tip O'Neill, in what has become an oft-quoted phrase. That simple truth can just as well be applied to Catholicism: it can also be said that "all faith is local"— that is to say, the Catholic faith is lived out and witnessed to powerfully, and often heroically, in the very concrete, daily, local, and ordinary lives of Catholics throughout this country.

In introducing the *Catechism of the Catholic Church*, Pope John Paul II encouraged the drafting of local catechisms in regions and countries throughout the world. He described the value of such local catechisms in this way: "The Universal Catechism is meant to encourage and assist in the writing of new local catechisms, which take into account various situations and cultures, while carefully preserving the unity of faith and fidelity to Catholic doctrine." (Apostolic Constitution, *Fidei Depositum,* 1992)

The *United States Catholic Catechism for Adults* is a response to this invitation. It is meant to enrich understanding and appropriation of the Universal Catechism, not replace or substitute for it. It presents Catholics with a renewed opportunity to study, reflect on and live by the faith we profess in the Creed, celebrate in the Sacraments, live in the Christian moral life, and deepen through prayer.

Why a National Catechism for Adults?

When we hear the words "Catechism" and "catechesis," we think almost immediately of the catechesis of children. Perhaps we recall our own childhood catechetical formation in CCD programs, in parish sacramental preparation programs, or the formal or informal catechesis we received growing up in the "domestic Church" that is a Catholic home.

While the catechetical formation of children and youth provides a necessary foundation for growth in faith in later years, the catechesis of adults is of vital significance. In recent years, various catechetical documents highlight the primary place of adult catechesis in the renewal of catechesis in our time. Taken together, they encourage a shift in our understanding of the nature of catechesis itself.

Pope John Paul II, for one, spoke clearly of the vital place of adult catechesis when he stressed, "adult catechesis is the *principal* form of catechesis, because it is addressed to persons who have the greatest responsibilities and the capacity to live the Christian message in its fully developed form" (*On Catechesis In Our Time,* 43). Similarly, the National Directory for Catechesis states that catechesis of adults should be "the '*organizing principle*' which gives coherence to the various catechetical programs offered by a particular Church . . . this is the axis around which revolves the catechesis of childhood and adolescence as well as that of old age" (48).

The catechetical formation of Catholic adults is essential for the Church to extend the mission entrusted by Christ to the apostles to proclaim the Gospel to the ends of the earth. All other forms of catechetical instruction — catechesis of children, youth, and young adults — depend on sound and effective adult catechesis. Without adult Catholics who are well formed in the essentials of faith, sacraments, prayer, and Christian living, there will be little or no effective catechesis of children, teens, and young adults.

The *United States Catholic Catechism for Adults* is written specifically for the ongoing catechetical formation of adults, to help Catholic adults in America continue to grow in faith in the person of Jesus Christ — as God's revealing love for the world — and to live in the power of the Holy Spirit, the Teacher of us all.

How to Use this Catechism Study Guide

The *United States Catholic Catechism for Adults* is composed of 36 chapters that follow the arrangement of the *Catechism of the Catholic Church*: Creed, Sacraments, Moral Life, and Prayer. The structure of each chapter includes the following elements:

1. Lessons or Stories of Faith
2. Teaching: Its Foundation and Application
3. Sidebars: Saints, Fathers, and Doctors of the Church
4. Relationship of Catholic Teaching to Culture

5. Discussion Questions
6. Doctrinal Statements
7. Meditation and Prayer

This Study Guide serves as a companion text, as it follows the outline of chapters of the *United States Catholic Catechism for Adults* so that you can easily move between both books. Chapters of the Study Guide are outlined this way:

• Summary of catechetical theme and application to culture
• Citations of relevant Scripture passages and references to the Universal Catechism and National Catechism
• Discussion questions based on the National Catechism
• Suggestions for further reading and study

Planning Your Catechetical Session
Introduction
Begin the catechetical session with a **Prayer to the Holy Spirit**:

Come, Holy Spirit, fill the hearts of your faithful, and kindle in us the fire of your love. Send forth your Spirit, and we shall be created, and You will renew the face of the earth. O God, who by the light of the Holy Spirit instructs the hearts of the faithful, grant that by that same Spirit we may be ever wise and rejoice in his consolations. We make our prayer in the name of Jesus Christ, our Lord. Amen.

Invite a participant to read one of the **Suggested Scripture Readings for Group Reflection** *(see the chapter you are studying)*.

Allow for a few moments of quiet recollection and reflection on Scripture to draw participants away from the distractions of the day and predispose their minds and hearts to receiving God's word (10 minutes).

Catechesis
Begin the catechetical moment by **reading** and **explaining** the **Summary** found in this Study Guide for the Chapter you are studying this week (15-20 minutes).

Read the **Story or Lesson of Faith** found in the *United States Catholic Catechism for Adults* for the chapter you are discussing (5 minutes).

Invite participants to share how the **Story or Lesson of Faith** illustrates the topic being discussed in this Chapter (10 minutes).

Application to Culture
Use the **Discussion Questions** (as needed) found in this Study Guide, based on questions in the *United States Catholic Catechism for Adults.* Discussion, whether in large or small groups, is an effective element of adult catechesis and serves to relate faith to life experience (10 minutes).

Conclusion

Conclude the catechetical session by reading the **Meditation** and **Prayer** found at the end of the chapter being discussed in the *United States Catholic Catechism for Adults.* Make participants aware of **suggestions for further reading and study** found at the end of each chapter of this Study Guide. The session may end with a suitable hymn (5 minutes).

✦ OUTLINE of CHAPTERS ✦

❖ *Chapter 1* ❖

MY SOUL LONGS FOR YOU, O GOD

INTRODUCTION

Prayer to the Holy Spirit, page 6

Choose one of the following Scripture readings:
- Ps. 105:1-15
- Acts 14:15-17
- Acts 17:26-28
- Rom. 1:19-20
- Wis. 13:1-9

Reflection Time

> **The *Catechism of the Catholic Church* and the Compendium**
>
> *CCC*: 27-49
> Compendium:
> Questions 1-5

CATECHESIS

Read this Summary:

To be human is to search for God. Throughout history, to the present moment, religious beliefs and practices express the human search for God. As creatures made in God's image and likeness, each one of us has been given a mind to search for the truth and a heart that longs for unconditional, forgiving love. These basic human desires are ultimately fulfilled in God, who is truth and love.

Your desire to know and understand the Catholic faith is *your* journey toward God through his Son, Jesus Christ, in the power of the Holy Spirit. Your desire for God is also an invitation to join in *our* common journey within the Church, the Body of Christ experienced as a living community of believers.

❖ All of us desire to live a fully human life.
❖ As human beings, we are religious beings with a longing for the infinite. This desire for God is written on every human heart because we are created by God for communion with God
❖ The dignity of every human being rests on the fact that we not only seek God but that God out of divine love invites us to enter into a personal relationship with him.
❖ Only in God do we find the full truth and happiness we continue searching for. To find truth and happiness in God is to find the complete fulfillment of our human desire for truth, love, and happiness.

Read the Lesson of Faith — St. Elizabeth Ann Seton in the *United States Catholic Catechism for Adults*, pages 1-2.

Reflection: How does the Lesson of Faith illustrate the topic of this session?

APPLICATION TO CULTURE

discussion

The following questions may be used to guide personal/group study and reflection along with the questions provided in the *United States Catholic Catechism for Adults,* page 7:

1. Discuss ways in which human beings tend to look for happiness apart from God? (*CCC* 29) Identify some illusory paths to happiness offered by popular culture.
2. How do we know that our search for true human happiness is a search for union with God? (*CCC* 27-30)
3. Where do we find evidence of God's desire for our human happiness? (*CCC* 31-35)
4. Share the path of your personal search for God till the present moment.
5. How can you concretely help others — family, friends, and neighbors — to overcome their doubts and fears as they search for God?

CONCLUSION

Read the Meditation and Prayer found in the *United States Catholic Catechism for Adults,* pages 8-9.

Make participants aware of the following suggestions for further reading and study:

A Time for Miracles (1980) DVD on St. Elizabeth Ann Seton.

Alma Power-Waters, *Mother Seton and the Sisters of Charity*. Ignatius Press, 2000.

St. Augustine, *Confessions*.

Joseph Cardinal Ratzinger, *Introduction to Christianity*. Ignatius Press, 2004.

Second Vatican Council, Pastoral Constitution on the Church in the Modern World (*Gaudium et Spes*), 4 -18.

Second Vatican Council, Declaration on Religious Freedom (*Dignitatis Humanae*), 1.

✣ *Chapter 2* ✣
GOD COMES TO MEET US

———

INTRODUCTION
Prayer to the Holy Spirit, page 6

Choose one of the following Scripture readings:
- Ps. 119:97-105
- Ex. 3:1-15; 4:10-16
- 1 Jn.1:2-3
- Eph.1:9; 2:18
- 2 Pet. 1:4

Reflection Time

> **The *Catechism of the Catholic Church* and the Compendium**
>
> *CCC*: 50-184
> Compendium:
> Questions 6-32

CATECHESIS
Read this Summary:

By natural reason, we can know God exists with certainty on the basis of the created world. Revelation is the love and knowledge of God that we cannot possibly arrive at by our own powers of reason. Out of divine love, God has chosen to reveal himself to the world. God's self-manifestation is the personal revelation of the mystery of his plan of salvation. The plan of divine revelation begins with creation and is perfectly fulfilled in the sending of God's own Son, Jesus Christ, for the redemption of the world.

Your reflection and study of the Catholic faith is an invitation to understand and accept the revelation of God in Jesus Christ in the power of the Holy Spirit. By revealing himself, God wishes to make each of us capable of responding to him, of knowing and loving him far beyond our own natural human capacity. Faith is the human response to God revealed.

❖ In love, God has revealed himself to humanity. Divine revelation provides the answers to the questions that human beings ask about the meaning and purpose of life (*CCC* 51-53).

❖ God reveals himself in order to invite us into friendship. God's will is that humanity should have access to the Father, through Jesus Christ, the Word made flesh, in the power of the Holy Spirit.

❖ God's revelation is manifested in words and deeds that have an inner unity. The stages of revelation begin with the creation of the world and continue with the covenant with Noah, the call of Abraham, and the people of Israel (*CCC* 54-67).

❖ God revealed himself fully by sending his own Son, Jesus Christ, in whom he has established his covenant forever.

❖ What Christ entrusted to his apostles, they handed on by their preaching and writing, under the inspiration of the Holy Spirit, to all generations till Christ's return in glory.

❖ Scripture and Tradition make up the single deposit of divine revelation (*CCC* 74-84).

❖ The task of interpreting the Word of God, whether in its written form or in the form of Tradition, has been entrusted to the living, teaching office of the Church. Its authority in this matter is exercised in the name of Jesus Christ. Bishops in communion with the successor of Peter, the Bishop of Rome interpret God's word (*CCC* 85).

Read the Lesson of Faith — Moses and the Burning Bush in the *United States Catholic Catechism for Adults*, pages 11-12.

Reflection: How does the Lesson of Faith illustrate the topic of this session?

APPLICATION TO CULTURE

Discussion

The following questions may be used to guide personal/group study and reflection along with the questions provided in the *United States Catholic Catechism for Adults,* page 17:

1. Why do human beings need God's revelation? (*CCC* 36-38)
2. Describe in your own words the main features of Christian revelation (*CCC* 51-53).
3. How does Scripture and Tradition mediate God's revelation through the Church to every baptized Christian? (*CCC* 74-84)
4. Identify ways in which Christian revelation differs from other world religions and from popular spirituality.
5. How is Christian revelation countercultural?

CONCLUSION

Read the Meditation and Prayer found in the *United States Catholic Catechism for Adults,* pages 18-19.

Make participants aware of the following suggestions for further reading and study:

Pope Benedict XVI, God Is Love (*Deus Caritas Est*), 2006.
Second Vatican Council, Dogmatic Constitution on Divine Revelation (*Dei Verbum*), 1-10.
Ex. 3:1-15; 4:10-16.
Col. 1:15.

Chapter 3

PROCLAIM THE GOSPEL TO EVERY CREATURE: THE TRANSMISSION OF DIVINE REVELATION

INTRODUCTION
Prayer to the Holy Spirit, page 6

Choose one of the following Scripture readings:
- Ps. 119:97-108
- 2 Tim. 3:14-17
- 1 Thess. 2:13

Reflection Time

The *Catechism of the Catholic Church* and the Compendium

CCC: 101-141
Compendium:
Questions 18-24

CATECHESIS
Read this Summary:
Christianity is a religion of the "Word of God," a living and Incarnate Word. In Apostolic Tradition and in the books of Sacred Scripture, God speaks to humanity in human words that are the "speech of God as it is put down in writing under the breath of the Holy Spirit" (*CCC* 81). Just as the Word of the eternal Father, Christ Jesus took human flesh, so are the words of God expressed in human words in the Sacred Scriptures.

Tradition is the "sacred deposit" of faith that Jesus Christ entrusted to the apostles who, in turn, through their preaching and teaching, hand on to the whole Church. In her doctrine, life, and worship, the Church hands on the fullness of this Apostolic Tradition to every generation. Sacred Tradition and Sacred Scripture "make up a single sacred deposit of the Word of God" (*Dei Verbum,* 10).

The Church honors the Scriptures as she honors the Lord's body. The Church presents to us the *one* bread of life, taken from the *one* table of God's Word and Christ's body at the Eucharistic altar. In Sacred Scripture, the Church constantly finds nourishment and strength, wisdom and hope, for believers welcome it not as a human word, "but as what it really is, the word of God" (1 Thess. 2:13).

The Bible (meaning "the book") is the most significant sacred text in human history. Translated into more languages than any other book, it is not just a storehouse of sublime teaching, sound wisdom for human life, and a treasury of prayers. It is the **revelation** of God's saving love unfolded in human history and the written record of God's fidelity in the face of human sinfulness. We approach the Bible with an attitude of faith, prayer, and study.

❖ The task of giving authentic interpretation of the Word of God, in its written form or in the form of Tradition, has been entrusted to the living, teaching office (*Magisterium*) of the Church. The Church, as the one who receives and hands on divine revelation, exercises this authority in the name of Jesus Christ.

❖ Church doctrines and dogmas are lights along the path of faith: they illumine it and make it secure. Our minds and hearts welcome the light of truth shed by doctrines and dogmas of faith (*CCC* 89).

❖ God is the author of Sacred Scripture "written under the inspiration of the Holy Spirit and handed down as such to the Church" (*CCC* 105).

❖ God inspired the human authors of the sacred books to teach humanity the truths of divine revelation. God chose sacred authors who "made full use of their own faculties and powers so that, though he acted in them and by them, it was as true authors that they consigned to writing whatever he wanted written, and no more" (*CCC* 107).

❖ Under the guidance of the Holy Spirit, the biblical authors record true accounts of salvation history, the messages of the prophets, the Wisdom sayings, the teachings and ministry of Jesus, his life, saving death and resurrection, and the experiences of the first Christians.

❖ The books of the Bible "firmly, faithfully, and without error teach that truth which God, for the sake of our salvation, wished to see confided to the Sacred Scriptures" (*CCC* 107).

❖ To interpret the Scriptures correctly, the reader must attend to what God desires to reveal to us and to what the human authors wanted to affirm. Sacred Scripture must be read and interpreted in the light of the same Spirit by whom it was written (*CCC* 109-110). The Church watches over and interprets the Word of God.

❖ The Church offers *three* criteria for interpreting Scripture: "the content and unity of the whole of Scripture," reading Scripture within the "living Tradition of the whole Church," and the "analogy of faith," or the coherence of truths of faith among themselves (*CCC* 112-114).

❖ The Church distinguishes between two senses of Scripture: the literal and the spiritual sense, further divided into the *allegorical,* the *moral,* and the *anagogical* (*CCC* 115-119).

❖ The list of sacred books is called the "canon" of Scripture. It includes 46 books for the Old Testament and 27 books for the New (*CCC* 120).

❖ The four Gospels — Matthew, Mark, Luke, and John — occupy a central place in the Church's life because "they are our principal source for the life and teaching of Jesus, the Incarnate Word" (*CCC* 124-127).

❖ The books of the Old Testament have permanent value in that the "Old Covenant has never been revoked." The unity of the two Testaments flows from the unity of God's plan for our salvation. The Old Testament prepares for the New Testament and the New fulfills the Old (*CCC* 128-130).

Read the Lesson of Faith — Blessed John XXIII in the *United States Catholic Catechism for Adults*, pages 21-22.

Reflection: How does the Lesson of Faith illustrate the topic of this session?

APPLICATION TO CULTURE

Discussion

The following questions may be used to guide personal/group study and reflection along with the questions provided in the *United States Catholic Catechism for Adults,* page 31:

1. Discuss the place of Sacred Tradition as you live out your faith (*CCC* 88-95).
2. How is the Bible a living source of faith for you?
3. How can you make reading and studying the Bible part of your daily prayer and spiritual reflection?
4. Reflect on the various meanings or "senses" of Scripture (*CCC* 115-118).
5. Discuss three conditions for interpreting Scripture with the guidance of the Holy Spirit who inspired it, as outlined in the *Catechism of the Catholic Church* (*CCC* 112-114).

CONCLUSION

Read the Meditation and Prayer found in the *United States Catholic Catechism for Adults,* pages 32-33.

Make participants aware of the following suggestions for further reading and study:

Journal of a Soul: The Autobiography of Pope John XXIII. Image Books, 1999.

Second Vatican Council, Dogmatic Constitution on Divine Revelation (*Dei Verbum*), Chapters II to VI.

Second Vatican Council, Dogmatic Constitution on the Sacred Liturgy (*Sacrosanctum Concilium*), 51.

Pontifical Biblical Commission, *The Interpretation of the Bible in the Church*, April 15, 1993.

Chapter 4

BRINGING ABOUT THE OBEDIENCE OF FAITH

INTRODUCTION
Prayer to the Holy Spirit, page 6

Choose one of the following Scripture readings:
- Ps. 130
- Heb. 11 and 12
- Rom. 3:21; 10:10; 16:26

Reflection Time

CATECHESIS
Read this summary:

God's revelation of love in Christ Jesus — in the power of the Holy Spirit — for our salvation, offers the possibility of a human response. Faith is the human response to God, who reveals. For Christians, faith is a free response of assent to the revelation of God, revealed in the Trinity of persons, Father, Son, and Holy Spirit. The Christian life is a relationship that begins with God's revelation in Christ Jesus and our response in faith to that revelation. Faith is a concrete gift from the Holy Spirit, who plants the seed of faith within us, nourishes and strengthens our faith and brings us to perfection in it.

St. Paul describes our human response to God's revelation as the *"obedience of faith"* (Rom.16:26) that is given freely and personally, within a community of believers. To "obey" (from the Latin *ob-audire,* to "hear" or "listen to") in faith is to freely embrace the Word of God as true because its truth is guaranteed by God. St. Paul also describes faith as the "assurance of things hoped for, the conviction of things not seen" (Heb.11:1).

The Scriptures offer us many models of faith beginning with Abraham, "our father in faith." Likewise, the Church through the ages proposes as saints those men and women whose living faith in Christ Jesus serves as a powerful example for us to imitate. Mary, the Mother of God, is the most perfect embodiment of faith in God's word. Through faith, we are linked to generations of believers from whom we receive faith so that we share it and witness to others as we live it.

In the midst of secular culture, living and defending one's faith is a gift and a challenge. For a Christian, faith is a personal *and* a communal act; it seeks greater understanding and engages our full

> **The *Catechism of the Catholic Church* and the Compendium**
>
> *CCC*: 142-184
> Compendium:
> Questions 24-32

powers of humanity; it is necessary for salvation as a gift that comes from the Holy Spirit, and it is a free, human act that believes with conviction in the truth of divine revelation in Christ Jesus.

❖ Faith is our personal and free assent to the whole truth of divine revelation (*CCC* 88-95). Faith is a gift from God, it is an ecclesial act, and it is necessary for our salvation (*CCC* 142-184).

❖ By faith we present our minds and our wills to God in the "obedience of faith." Faith may be defined as the "assurance of things hoped for, the conviction of things not seen" (Heb.11:1).

❖ The Catholic Church looks to Mary, the Mother of Christ, as the purest realization of faith. The Virgin Mary perfectly embodies the obedience of faith as she welcomed the message of the Archangel Gabriel, who announced the coming of Christ, believing that "with God nothing will be impossible" (*CCC* 148-149).

❖ Christian faith is Trinitarian and Christ-centered; in faith we put our free and full trust in God alone, in Jesus Christ, the Son of God, and in the Holy Spirit. The Church never ceases to proclaim faith in one God: Father, Son, and Holy Spirit (*CCC* 150-152).

❖ Faith is a gift from God, who moves our heart, mind, and will to know, love, and serve him. In order to believe in God's word, we need the interior help of the Holy Spirit.

❖ To "believe" is a human act, conscious and free, that corresponds to the dignity of being made in the image and likeness of God, our Creator.

❖ Faith seeks understanding so that, with the light of reason, we may understand the mystery of God's plan of salvation in Christ Jesus. Faith is not a blind impulse of the mind; rather, faith and reason lead us to deeper knowledge and contemplation of God.

❖ To "believe" is a personal and communal act — above all, faith is an "ecclesial" act. We receive the life of faith through the Church in Baptism, Confirmation, and the Eucharist, and are sustained for the journey of faith by God's word and sacraments. The faith of the Church precedes, strengthens, sustains, and nourishes our faith (*CCC* 168-169).

❖ Faith is necessary for salvation. The Word of God and the sacraments of the Church nourish and sustain us to live, grow, and persevere in faith till the end.

Read the Lesson of Faith — Fr. Isaac Thomas Hecker in the *United States Catholic Catechism for Adults*, pages 35-36.

Reflection: How does the Lesson of Faith illustrate the topic of this session?

APPLICATION TO CULTURE

Discussion

The following questions may be used to guide personal/group study and reflection along with the questions provided in the *United States Catholic Catechism for Adults*, page 44:

1. Reflect on and share how you received faith from the Church. Why is the "ecclesial" dimension of faith important?
2. Identify challenges posed by popular culture to people of faith.
3. How does the full "obedience of faith" help us respond to these cultural challenges?
4. What concrete and ongoing steps do you take to daily grow and be nourished in faith by God's word and the sacraments?
5. How do you share your Christian faith with others — family, friends, neighbors, co-workers?

CONCLUSION

Read the Meditation and Prayer found in the *United States Catholic Catechism for Adults,* pages 45-47.

Make participants aware of the following suggestions for further reading and study:

Isaac T. Hecker, the Diary: Romantic Religion in Ante-Bellum America (Sources of American Spirituality).

Second Vatican Council, Dogmatic Constitution on Divine Revelation (*Dei Verbum*), Chapters I and II.

Pope John Paul II, Faith and Reason (*Fides et Ratio*), 1998.

John Henry Cardinal Newman, *Apologia pro vita sua.* London: Longman, 1878.

Chapter 5

I BELIEVE IN GOD

INTRODUCTION
Prayer to the Holy Spirit, page 6

Choose one of the following Scripture readings:
- Ps. 8
- 1 Jn. 4:7-12

Reflection Time

CATECHESIS
Read this Summary:

The *Catechism of the Catholic Church* and the Compendium

CCC: 199-349
Compendium:
Questions 36-65

We begin the Christian Creed by professing belief in God, the "Father Almighty, Creator of heaven and earth." This is the starting point for the whole symphony of Christian belief — in God, who is Father, Son, and Holy Spirit. All the other articles of the Creed depend on the first article of the Creed and give concrete meaning to it. The mystery of God who is a Trinity of Persons is the central mystery of Christian faith and life.

To believe in God as a Christian is to believe that the Trinity of divine persons is One, that each divine Person is distinct from the other, and that the divine Persons are related to one another in a divine community of love. Every Christian is baptized in the name of the Triune God — in the name of the Father, and of the Son, and of the Holy Spirit.

God, who is always transcendent and beyond complete human comprehension, has lovingly revealed himself to humanity in the history of salvation. God is revealed as Creator in the opening verses of Scripture, "In the beginning when God created the heavens and the earth" (Gen.1:1).

In sending his only Son, Christ Jesus, into the world, God's saving plan of redemption was revealed to humanity. The Holy Spirit, given to the Church at Pentecost, inspires and sustains the Church to continue Christ's loving work of salvation, healing, and reconciliation to God.

- ❖ The mystery of the Holy Trinity of God is the central mystery of Christian faith and of Christian life (*CCC* 261).
- ❖ God is a holy mystery; not a "mystery" to be solved as a riddle or puzzle, but a divine truth that invites us to communion, friendship, and unconditional love.

❖ The Old Testament reveals God who is One, unique and without equal (Deut. 6:4; Mk. 12:29). In Genesis, God is revealed as the Creator of the world, the Almighty and eternal Truth of all that exists.

❖ God alone reveals himself as Father, Son, and Holy Spirit. Christ Jesus reveals God as his Father and promises the Holy Spirit as our teacher, guide, and comforter.

❖ To profess belief in God, as a Christian, is to entrust oneself to God's love and providence, by which God guides all creatures with wisdom and love.

❖ Angels are spiritual creatures who glorify God and work for our salvation. The Church venerates angels who guide and protect every human being. (*CCC* 328-351)

Read the Lesson of Faith — Orestes Brownson in the *United States Catholic Catechism for Adults*, pages 49-50.

Reflection: How does the Lesson of Faith illustrate the topic of this session?

APPLICATION TO CULTURE

Discussion

The following questions may be used to guide personal/group study and reflection along with the questions provided in the *United States Catholic Catechism for Adults*, page 61:

1. What does faith in God mean to you personally?
2. What does it mean to be "created in the image and likeness of God?"
3. Why does the Creed begin with God? (*CCC* 198)
4. Discuss the implications of believing in a God who is a Trinity of divine Persons — Father, Son, and Holy Spirit (*CCC* 222-227).
5. How is your life shaped by your Christian belief that "God is love" (1 Jn. 4:8)?

CONCLUSION

Read the Meditation and Prayer found in the *United States Catholic Catechism for Adults, page* 63.

Make participants aware of the following suggestions for further reading and study:

Orestes A. Brownson, *Selected Writings* (Sources of American Spirituality).

Second Vatican Council, Pastoral Constitution on the Church in the Modern World (*Gaudium et Spes*), 1-18.

Chapter 6
MAN AND WOMAN IN THE BEGINNING

INTRODUCTION
Prayer to the Holy Spirit, page 6

Choose one of the following Scripture readings:
- Gen. 1:1-2, 27-28
- Ps. 8
- Ps. 104: 24

Reflection Time

CATECHESIS
Read this Summary:

The Bible opens with these words: "In the beginning . . . God created the heavens and the earth" (Gen. 1:1). The first three chapters of the first book of the Bible focus on creation: its origins and destiny in God, its beauty and order, the creation of human beings, the drama of sin, and the hope of salvation.

The origins of the world and human race are among the most basic riddles of human existence. Science studies such questions, enriching our knowledge of the universe and the development of life, and then offers theories on when and how the universe arose and human beings appeared. However, within every culture, there remain questions beyond those that can be answered by scientific research.

What is the meaning and purpose of our origins? Why do we exist at all? Where are we going? If the world was created out of God's goodness, why is there evil? Questions about our origin and our end are inseparable. They determine the meaning, purpose, and direction of human life.

What we believe about the creation of the world and of humanity, and about our relationship with God, the Creator, is of vital importance. It points us to the foundations of the Christian life.

- ❖ The creation of the world by a loving God is the foundation of "all God's saving plans" (*CCC* 280). Creation begins the history of salvation that culminates in Jesus Christ.
- ❖ The first three chapters of Genesis teach the truths of creation: its origin and its end in a loving God, its order and goodness, the vocation of man and woman, and finally the drama of sin and the hope of salvation (*CCC* 289).

> **The *Catechism of the Catholic Church* and the Compendium**
>
> *CCC*: 279-324, 385-421
> Compendium:
> Questions 51-58, 73-78

❖ We believe that God created the world freely and out of love to make his creatures share in his goodness and happiness. The world is not the product of chance or blind fate (*CCC* 295).

❖ Creation is ordered and it is good; with creation, God does not abandon creatures to themselves. God creates out of nothing, giving existence to the world, and at every moment he sustains and upholds creation in being (*CCC* 299-301, 319-320).

❖ Man and woman are created as the crown of creation — we are created as material and spiritual beings. We are body and soul, created in the image of God.

❖ The existence of physical and moral evil is a mystery that God illuminates by his Son, Jesus, who died and rose to overcome evil (*CCC* 324).

❖ Original Sin is "a deprivation of original holiness and justice, but human nature is not totally corrupted; it is wounded in the natural powers proper to it" (*CCC* 405, 396-401).

❖ Due to Original Sin, humanity is subject to ignorance, suffering, and the dominion of death; and inclined to sin — an inclination to evil that is called "concupiscence" (*CCC* 405).

❖ Sin is humanity's rejection of God's love. Sin breaks the bonds of friendship with God and with one another.

Read the Lesson of Faith — Rose Hawthorne Lathrop (Mother Alphonsa) in the *United States Catholic Catechism for Adults*, pages 65-67.

Reflection: How does the Lesson of Faith illustrate the topic of this session?

APPLICATION TO CULTURE

Discussion

The following questions may be used to guide personal/group study and reflection along with the questions provided in the *United States Catholic Catechism for Adults*, pages 72-73:

1. Discuss the consequences of believing that every human person is "created in the image and likeness of God."
2. How is the biblical understanding of the creation of the world and human persons different from other worldviews? (*CCC* 285)
3. How do scientific theories of evolution relate to Scripture? (*CCC* 283-289)
4. What effect does sin have on us as individuals? On our relationship with others, on culture, on the world?
5. What is God's response to human sinfulness?

CONCLUSION

Read the Meditation and Prayer found in the *United States Catholic Catechism for Adults*, pages 74-75.

Make participants aware of the following suggestions for further reading and study:

Rose Hawthorne Lathrop: Selected Writings (Sources of American Spirituality).

Second Vatican Council, Pastoral Constitution on the Church in the Modern World (*Gaudium et Spes)*, 1-18.

Pope John Paul II, *Original Unity of Man and Woman*, 1979.

Chapter 7

THE GOOD NEWS:
GOD HAS SENT HIS SON

INTRODUCTION
Prayer to the Holy Spirit, page 6

Choose one of the following Scripture readings:
- Jn. 1:14, 16
- 1 Jn. 1:1-4
- Phil. 2:5-8
- Gal. 4:4-5
- Heb.10:5-7

Reflection Time

> **The *Catechism of the Catholic Church* and the Compendium**
>
> *CCC*: 422-682
> Compendium:
> Questions 79-135

CATECHESIS
Read this Summary:

"God so loved the world that he sent his only begotten Son, so that whoever believes in him should not perish but have eternal life" (Jn. 3:16). The heart of Christian belief is the Incarnation of God in the person of Jesus Christ, who we believe is the Son of God sent into the world.

All the promises God made in the history of salvation — from Adam and Eve, to Abraham, Moses, and David, to the prophets and kings of Israel — come to fulfillment in the life, death, and resurrection of Jesus Christ. The history of salvation reaches its completion in the person of the "Word Made Flesh," Jesus Christ, the Son of God.

As the Word of God made visible in human form, Christ Jesus fully reveals God's love and saving plan for humanity. In Christ each of us discovers our full human dignity as creatures made in the image and likeness of God and redeemed by the 'Word made flesh." In the life, death and resurrection of Christ we understand the deepest meaning and purpose of our existence as children of God.

The Word was made flesh so that we might know God's love and be reconciled to God. We believe that Christ Jesus is not only a great teacher, prophet, liberator, and founder of the Christian faith. He is the Incarnation of God, the "invisible made visible," true God and true man, God's only Son.

❖ Central to Christian faith is belief in the mystery of the "Incarnation," by which the Son of God assumed a human nature in order to accomplish our salvation in it. In the Incarnation, God the Father reveals the Son in the power of the Holy Spirit. (*CCC* 461-463).

❖ The unique and altogether singular event of the Incarnation of the Son of God does not mean that Jesus is part God and part man. Nor is he a mixture of the divine and the human. Jesus became truly man while remaining truly God: he is true God and true man. The Incarnation is the mystery of the union between the divine and human natures in the one person of Christ, the "Word made flesh" (*CCC* 464).

❖ Jesus is the one mediator between God and man. During the early centuries, the Church had to defend and clarify this central Christian belief against numerous opposing views (*CCC* 464-469).

❖ The Gospels give us the record of the whole life of Christ from his birth, his miracles and teachings, his examples of love and compassion, to his passion and death on the cross and his glorious resurrection.

❖ The "Word became flesh" in Christ to be our model of love, forgiveness and holiness. "Love one another as I have loved you" (Jn.15:12). To be a disciple of Christ is to love God and to imitate Jesus' actions as we follow his teachings of love, mercy and compassion for others.

❖ The names given to Jesus tell us about his mission and his work for our salvation: "Jesus" means "God saves" (*CCC* 430-435); the word "Christ" means "Messiah" or the One Anointed and chosen by God (*CCC* 436-440); the title "Son of God" reflects his divine origin and identity; and the name "Lord" indicates his divine power over the world. (*CCC* 446-451).

❖ The Church believes that the "key, the center, and the purpose of the whole of human history is to be found in Jesus Christ" (*CCC* 450).

❖ The chief mysteries of Christ's life are his birth, the "Paschal mystery" of his sufferings and death on the Cross, and his victory over sin and death in the resurrection (*CCC* 512-658).

❖ "The whole of Christ's life was a continual teaching: his silences, his miracles, his gestures, his prayer, his love for people, his special affection for the little and the poor, his acceptance of the total sacrifice on the Cross for the redemption of the world, and his Resurrection are the fulfillment of divine Revelation" (*CCC* 561).

Read the Lesson of Faith — Ven. Pierre Toussaint in the *United States Catholic Catechism for Adults*, pages 77-79.

Reflection: How does the Lesson of Faith illustrate the topic of this session?

APPLICATION TO CULTURE
Discussion
The following questions may be used to guide personal/group study and reflection along with the questions provided in the *United States Catholic Catechism for Adults,* page 85:

1. Why is belief in Jesus Christ as the Son of God — and not merely as a wise teacher or social liberator — so central to Christian faith?
2. How can you deepen your personal relationship with Christ? Identify concrete ways you can grow in your participation in the mystery of Jesus' life, his teachings and his saving death and resurrection.

3. "Who do you say that I am?" is Jesus' question to his disciples. Peter answers, "You are the Christ, the Son of the living God" (Mt. 16:16). How would you answer Jesus' question — "Who do you say that I am?"

4. If God took on our human nature in the Incarnation of Jesus, what does that say about the dignity of our human nature?

5. How does the Good News of the Incarnation help us respond to challenges to faith posed by culture today?

CONCLUSION

Read the Meditation and Prayer found in the *United States Catholic Catechism for Adults,* pages 86-87.

Make participants aware of the following suggestions for further reading and study:

Arthur Jones*, Pierre Toussaint: A Biography.* Doubleday, 2003.

Second Vatican Council, Dogmatic Constitution on Divine Revelation (*Dei Verbum*), Chapter I.

Pope John Paul II, The Redeemer of Man (*Redemptor Hominis*). Encyclical Letter, March 4, 1979.

Chapter 8

THE SAVING DEATH AND RESURRECTION OF CHRIST

INTRODUCTION
Prayer to the Holy Spirit, page 6

Choose one of the following Scripture readings:
- Mt.16:21-23
- Mt. 17:22-23
- Lk. 9:23
- 1 Jn. 4:9

Reflection Time

The *Catechism of the Catholic Church* and the Compendium

CCC: 571-664
Compendium:
Questions 112-132

CATECHESIS
Read this Summary:

The Paschal Mystery is the saving death and resurrection of Jesus for the redemption of the world. It is a core Christian belief that by his death on the cross and his resurrection from the dead, Jesus overcame death and sin. The Paschal Mystery of Christ offers to each of us the fruits of his redemptive work and stands at the center of the Good News of the Gospel.

The liturgy celebrates the Paschal Mystery, above all, in the "Sacred Triduum" of Holy Thursday, Good Friday, and the Easter Vigil. On Holy Thursday, by instituting the Eucharist, Jesus anticipates his dying and rising from the dead. Jesus' death on the cross and his Resurrection are bound together as one redemptive action of divine love for the salvation of the world.

By his death on the cross, Jesus overcame sin and death. In rising, he brings new life, grace, and the Holy Spirit, so we might know the dignity of being adopted as sons and daughters of God. Humanity needs salvation from sin and death and the strength of new life in Christ. In Baptism, we die to sin with Christ and are raised to new life in the Holy Spirit. This dying and rising with Christ is our participation in the Paschal Mystery.

❖ The Paschal Mystery of Christ's cross and Resurrection stands at the center of the Good News of the Gospel that the apostles and the Church after them, proclaims to the world (*CCC* 571). This mystery of faith is proclaimed in the words of the Creed.

❖ God's saving plan was accomplished "once and for all" in the redeeming death of his Son Jesus Christ, who came from God to do the will of God.

❖ Jesus' death on the cross is both the Paschal sacrifice that accomplishes the definitive redemption of men and the sacrifice of the New Covenant that restores humanity to communion with God. The Paschal Mystery is unique; it completes and surpasses all sacrifices. It overcomes the effects of our disobedience to God and is the means of our reconciliation with God (*CCC* 613-614).

❖ The Paschal Mystery is the manifestation of God's love in his Son, who pours out his life on the cross for our sins. Jesus substitutes his obedience for our human disobedience and reveals his divine love as a unique source of eternal salvation (*CCC* 599-618).

❖ We participate in the Paschal mystery through the sacraments, especially Baptism and the Eucharist. In Baptism, we die and rise with Christ to a new life in the Holy Spirit. In the Eucharist, we are united with Christ's unique offering on the cross, sacramentally present in every Eucharistic sacrifice.

❖ Christ's resurrection is an event historically attested to by the apostles, who met their risen Lord. The reality of Christ's resurrection is also a transcendent event beyond the realm of human history. The apostolic witness to Christ's Resurrection is the foundation of the Church's proclamation of the Paschal Mystery to the world (*CCC* 638-658).

❖ We believe that Christ Jesus ascended to heaven and he will come at the end of time in glory to judge the living and the dead (*CCC* 659-682).

Read the Lesson of Faith — Sr. Thea Bowman in the *United States Catholic Catechism for Adults*, pages 89-90.

Reflection: How does the Lesson of Faith illustrate the topic of this session?

APPLICATION TO CULTURE
Discussion
The following questions may be used to guide personal/group study and reflection along with the questions provided in the *United States Catholic Catechism for Adults,* page 98:

1. Why is belief in the Paschal Mystery of Christ's cross and resurrection central to faith as a Christian? (Read 1 Cor. 15:14, 17.)
2. Reflect on daily ways in which you participate in the mystery of Jesus' cross and Resurrection.
3. How do you unite challenges and hardships with the sufferings of Christ on the cross? How do you experience the new life of his resurrection?
4. Identify common obstacles to belief in Christ's resurrection.
5. Why did Jesus need to suffer and die for the salvation of humanity?

CONCLUSION
Read the Meditation and Prayer found in the *United States Catholic Catechism for Adults*, pages 99-100.

Make participants aware of the following suggestions for further reading and study:

Sister Thea Bowman, FSPA, and Margaret Walker, *God Touched My Life: The Inspiring Autobiography of the Nun Who Brought Song, Celebration, and Soul to the World.* HarperCollins, 1992.

Scripture Readings and Liturgy of Holy Thursday, Good Friday, and the Easter Vigil.

Pope John Paul II, The Redeemer of Man (*Redemptor Hominis*), March 4, 1979.

Documents of the Second Vatican Council, Dogmatic Constitution on the Church (*Lumen Gentium*), 1-5.

Chapter 9

RECEIVE THE HOLY SPIRIT

----------◆◆◆----------

INTRODUCTION

Prayer to the Holy Spirit, page 6

Choose one of the following Scripture readings:

- Is.11:1-2
- Jn. 6:13; 14:16, 26
- Gal. 3:14
- Rom. 8:15
- Acts 2:1-4

Reflection Time

> **The *Catechism of the Catholic Church* and the Compendium**
>
> *CCC:* 683-747
> Compendium:
> Questions 136-146

CATECHESIS

Read this Summary:

The Holy Spirit is God, the third divine Person of the Trinity, sometimes called the *Paraclete*, an Advocate and Comforter, the Lord and Giver of Life. At the Last Supper, Jesus promised to send the Holy Spirit: "I will send him to you" (Jn. 16:7). After his death, resurrection, and ascension into heaven, Jesus sends the Holy Spirit upon the Church to inspire, strengthen, and vivify God's people.

The Holy Spirit is poured out at Pentecost (meaning fiftieth day) to sanctify the Church and to continue the abiding presence of Christ among us. In the Acts of the Apostles and the New Testament epistles, we trace the work of the Holy Spirit in the Church. The Spirit sanctifies and strengthens believers to live a new life in Christ and to proclaim the Good News to the world.

We come to know the Holy Spirit within the community of the Church, in the Scriptures inspired by the Spirit, in the Tradition of the Church's teachings and doctrines, in the sacraments — particularly the Eucharist — and in prayer, apostolates, and ministries that build up the Body of Christ.

At our Baptism, the Holy Spirit removes Original Sin and incorporates us into the Body of Christ. At Confirmation, the Holy Spirit strengthens us to proclaim, in word and deed, the Good News of the Gospel. At every Eucharist, the Holy Spirit transforms the bread and wine into the Body and Blood of Christ through the ministry of the priest. When we are open, the Holy Spirit continually converts and transforms us into dwelling places for Christ to live as children of God.

❖ To believe in the Holy Spirit is to profess that the Holy Spirit is the third Person of the Holy Trinity, of the same substance as the Father and the Son. The Holy Spirit is at work with the Father and the Son from the beginning to the end of salvation history (*CCC* 685-686).

❖ The titles of the Holy Spirit include the "Paraclete," which means "he who is called to one's side," an *ad-vocatu,* and "the Spirit of truth" (Jn. 16:13). St. Paul uses such titles as "The Spirit of adoption," "the Spirit of the Lord," and the "Spirit of Christ" (*CCC* 692-693).

❖ The symbols of the Holy Spirit include the sacramental signs of water, anointing, fire, cloud and light, seal, hand or finger of God, and the dove. (*CCC* 694-701).

❖ By the action of the Holy Spirit in Mary, the Mother of God, all the preparations and promises of Christ's coming are completed. By the action of the Holy Spirit in her, God gives us "Emmanuel," "God-with-us" (Mt.1:23) (*CCC* 721-726).

❖ At Pentecost, the Holy Trinity is fully revealed when Jesus' Paschal Mystery is fulfilled in the outpouring of the Holy Spirit (*CCC* 731-736).

❖ The gifts of the Holy Spirit are: Wisdom, Understanding, Counsel (Right Judgment), Fortitude (Courage), Knowledge, Piety (Reverence), and Fear of the Lord. The fruits of the Holy Spirit (Gal. 5:22-23) are: Love, Joy, Peace, Patience, Kindness, Goodness, Generosity, Gentleness, Faithfulness, Modesty, Self-Control, and Chastity (*CCC* 736, 1831-1832).

❖ The Holy Spirit opens our hearts and minds to experience God in numerous ways: in reading and praying with Scripture; in reading the lives of the saints; in assenting to the teachings of the Magisterium, in our active participation in the sacraments; in daily personal prayer; in missionary or apostolic efforts; in charisms and ministries that build the Church; and in the Tradition of the Church (*CCC* 688).

❖ The Holy Spirit builds the Church through gifts and ministries and is the master of prayer, the one who teaches us how to pray (*CCC* 737-741).

Read the Lesson of Faith — Bl. Kateri Tekakwitha in the *United States Catholic Catechism for Adults*, pages 101-102.

Reflection: How does the Lesson of Faith illustrate the topic of this session?

APPLICATION TO CULTURE

Discussion

The following questions may be used to guide personal/group study and reflection along with the questions provided in the *United States Catholic Catechism for Adults*, page 108:

1. Share your experience of the grace and gifts of the Holy Spirit.
2. How are the gifts and fruits of the Holy Spirit manifested in the Church and in your community of faith?
3. What gifts of the Holy Spirit do you offer for the building up of Christ's Body?
4. How can you grow in holiness with the fruits of the Holy Spirit?
5. Recall the graces you received in the Sacrament of Confirmation; do you rely on the grace of the Holy Spirit every day?

CONCLUSION

Read the Meditation and Prayer found in the *United States Catholic Catechism for Adults,* pages 109-110.

Make participants aware of the following suggestions for further reading and study:

Margaret Bunson, *Kateri Tekakwitha, Mystic of the Wilderness.* Our Sunday Visitor, 1998.

Second Vatican Council, Dogmatic Constitution on the Church (*Lumen Gentium*), 1-15.

Pope John Paul II, The Lord and Giver of Life (*Dominum et Vivificantem*), May 18, 1986.

Pope John Paul II, Lay Members of Christ's Faithful (*Christifideles Laici*), December 30, 1988.

St. Basil, *On the Holy Spirit.*

The Rite of Confirmation.

Chapter 10

THE CHURCH: REFLECTING THE LIGHT OF CHRIST

INTRODUCTION
Prayer to the Holy Spirit, page 6

Choose one of the following Scripture readings:
- Acts 2:43-47
- Mt. 16:18
- Jn. 17:21
- Eph. 4:3-5

Reflection Time

> **The *Catechism of the Catholic Church* and the Compendium**
>
> *CCC*: 748-975
> Compendium:
> Questions 147-199

CATECHESIS
Read this Summary:

The word "Church" (Latin *ecclesia*) originally meant a gathering or assembly. In Christian usage, the word "church" refers to the worshipping community, the local community (or "parish"), and the entire universal community of believers (*CCC* 751-752).

In the Old Testament, God called the chosen people of Israel to be his holy people. The first Christians saw themselves as a continuation of that assembly. God created the world for communion with divine life, and the Church is that community founded by Jesus Christ through which we grow in communion with God and with one another. In the Church, God now calls together all people into one community of faith, hope, and love. God calls us and forms us into a community of love, not as isolated individuals. The Church is a worldwide institution; it is a community of love, sharing faith in Christ Jesus in the common hope of eternal salvation.

The Church was inaugurated by Jesus' preaching and teaching and by his choice of twelve apostles with Peter as the head of the community. Ultimately, the mystery of the visible and invisible reality of the Church is born from Jesus' total self-giving on the Cross. The mystery of the Church is that her origin is in the communion of divine persons in the Trinity — the Church possesses both divine and human elements, a visible society and a spiritual reality. The Church has no other light than the light of Christ.

❖ The Church is a holy *mystery*, because her origin is in the communion of the Father, the Son, and the Holy Spirit. The Father called the Church into existence, Christ founded the Church, and the Holy Spirit fills the Church with power and wisdom at Pentecost and in every age (*CCC* 758-769).

❖ The Church is a holy *mystery* — both "visible" and "spiritual," divine and human, the earthly Church and the heavenly community, a hierarchically ordered institution and the mystical Body of Christ (*CCC* 770-780).

❖ The Church is the *sacrament of our salvation*, the sign and instrument of our communion and relationship with God (*CCC* 774-776).

❖ The Church is the *People of God*. We become members of God's people through faith in Jesus Christ and in Baptism (*CCC* 781-786).

❖ The Church is the *Body of Christ*, with Christ as the Head and us as the members (*CCC* 787-795).

❖ The Church is the *Temple of the Holy Spirit* who sanctifies her members and pours out abundant gifts and charisms for the building up of the Church (*CCC* 797-801).

❖ The Church is a *communion* that begins with our union with Christ Jesus. Through the communion of the Church, we are given a share in the communion of the Trinity and drawn into a community of faith, hope, and love with all men and women (*CCC* 813, 948, 959).

Read the Lesson of Faith — The Apostle Peter in the *United States Catholic Catechism for Adults*, pages 111-112.

Reflection: How does the Lesson of Faith illustrate the topic of this session?

APPLICATION TO CULTURE

Discussion

The following questions may be used to guide personal/group study and reflection along with the questions provided in the *United States Catholic Catechism for Adults*, page 121:

1. What are the consequences of believing that the Church is a mystery — with divine and human elements, visible and spiritual — holy, yet made up of sinful members?

2. What does it mean to belong to the People of God? How does the Church as a communion of love shape your faith?

3. What are the implications of believing that Christ founded the Church, and that he is the Head of his Body, of which we are members?

4. What do the biblical images of the Church as Body of Christ, sheepfold, cultivated field, and temple mean to you?

5. What are some common cultural misperceptions about the Catholic Church? How do you respond to them?

CONCLUSION

Read the Meditation and Prayer found in the *United States Catholic Catechism for Adults*, page 123.

Make participants aware of the following suggestions for further reading and study:

Joseph Cardinal Ratzinger, *Pilgrim Fellowship of Faith*. Ignatius Press, 2005.

Second Vatican Council, Dogmatic Constitution on the Church (*Lumen Gentium*), Chapter I, 1-8.

Pope John Paul II, On the Eucharist in Its Relationship to the Church (*Ecclesia de Eucharistia*), Chapters I–III.

Chapter 11

THE FOUR MARKS OF THE CHURCH

INTRODUCTION
Prayer to the Holy Spirit, page 6

Choose one of the following Scripture readings:
- Acts 2:43-47
- Jn. 17:21
- Eph. 4:3-5
- Mt. 16:18

Reflection Time

CATECHESIS
Read this Summary:

> **The *Catechism of the Catholic Church* and the Compendium**
>
> *CCC*: 811-870
> Compendium:
> Questions 161-176

In the words of the Creed, we profess "one, holy, catholic, and apostolic Church." These four characteristics, or "marks," affirm the essential features of the Catholic Church, her origin, and her mission in the world. The Church does not possess these characteristics; rather, we believe that it is Christ who, through the power of the Holy Spirit, makes his Body, the Church, "one, holy, catholic, and apostolic."

❖ Jesus Christ makes the Church "one, holy, catholic, and apostolic." Only in fidelity to Jesus' teachings and his saving mission can the Church realize fully each of these qualities (*CCC* 811-822).

❖ The Church is one because of her founder and source: Jesus Christ. But from its very beginning, the one Church is marked by a diversity that comes from the variety of gifts and the diversity of those who receive them. Among the Church's members there are different gifts, offices, conditions, and ways of life (*CCC* 813-815).

❖ The oneness of the Church is held together by "bonds of unity" or visible bonds of communion which are: above all charity, the profession of one faith received from the apostles, common celebration of the sacraments, and apostolic succession through Holy Orders (*CCC* 815).

❖ The "sole Church of Christ is that which our Savior entrusted to Peter's pastoral care, commissioning him and the other apostles to extend and pastor it . . . this Church, constituted and organized as a society in this present world, *subsists* in the Catholic Church, governed by the successor of Peter and by bishops in communion with him. Elements of sanctification and truth are also found outside its visible confines" (*CCC* 816).

❖ From the beginning, divisions arose in the Church. Through the centuries, large communities of Christians became separated from full communion — for which people of all sides were to blame. These divisions in the Body of Christ are a wound to Christian unity and contrary to the will of Christ (*CCC* 817-822).

❖ The Church is the holy People of God made holy by Christ, her founder. While holy the Church is composed of sinful members who are constantly in need of conversion (*CCC* 825-827).

❖ From time to time the Church *canonizes* saints, in whom the holiness of the Church shines. In canonizing saints, the Church recognizes God's sanctifying power in the lives of holy men and women and offers them to us as models of Christian living. (*CCC* 828-829).

❖ The Church is catholic, meaning universal. Christ is present in the Church; she proclaims the fullness of faith to all peoples and is present everywhere in the world (*CCC* 830-856).

❖ The Church is apostolic in that she is founded on the faith of the apostles. She continues to be taught, sanctified, and guided by the successors of the apostles, the bishops, assisted by priests, in union with the successor of Peter, the Pope (*CCC* 857-865).

Read the Lesson of Faith — Bl. Junípero Serra in the *United States Catholic Catechism for Adults*, pages 125-126.

Reflection: How does the Lesson of Faith illustrate the topic of this session?

APPLICATION TO CULTURE
Discussion

The following questions may be used to guide personal/group study and reflection along with the questions provided in the *United States Catholic Catechism for Adults,* page 137:

1. Share insights you have gained from reflecting on the "marks" of the Church as "one, holy, catholic, and apostolic."

2. Just as we honor people of heroic virtue and extraordinary abilities in society, the Church honors the saints as "heroes of holiness." Discuss one example of a Christian saint whose serves as a model of holiness to you.

3. On the eve of his passion and death, Jesus prayed for the unity of his disciples with these words: ". . . that they may all be one; even as thou, Father, art in me and I in thee, that they also may be in us" (Jn.17:21). Why are efforts toward Christian unity among believers important today?

CONCLUSION
Read the Meditation and Prayer found in the *United States Catholic Catechism for Adults, page* 139.

Make participants aware of the following suggestions for further reading and study:
M. N. L. Couve De Murville, *The Man Who Founded California: The Life of Blessed Junípero Serra*. Ignatius Press, 2000.
Second Vatican Council, Dogmatic Constitution on the Church (*Lumen Gentium*), Chapter I, 1-8.
Pope John Paul II, On the Eucharist in its Relationship to the Church (*Ecclesia de Eucharistia*), Chapters 3 and 4, 26-46.
Pope Pius XII, The Mystical Body of Christ (*Mystici Corporis*), 1943.

Chapter 12
MARY: THE CHURCH'S FIRST AND MOST PERFECT MEMBER

INTRODUCTION
Prayer to the Holy Spirit, page 6

Choose one of the following Scripture readings:
- Lk. 1:26-38 (Annunciation)
- Lk. 1:46-55 (Magnificat)
- Mt. 1:18-25
- Jn. 16:14-15; 19:26-27
- 1 Cor. 1:17
- Heb. 3:6

Reflection Time

The *Catechism of the Catholic Church* and the Compendium

CCC: 484-511; 963-975
Compendium:
Questions 94-100;
196-199

CATECHESIS
Read this Summary:

Catholic beliefs about Mary and the saints are based on what is believed about Jesus Christ and the Church. Christ Jesus, as the Son of God, is fully human and fully divine. And Mary, the Mother of the Son of God, occupies a special and unique place in God's plan of salvation.

From ancient times to the present day, Catholics honor the unique role of Mary, the woman chosen to be the Mother of our Redeemer, with a special reverence and devotion. We do not adore or worship Mary; adoration and worship is given only to God, to Jesus Christ, and to the Holy Spirit. We venerate her singular example and prayerfully request her intercession for us.

Mary, at the message of the Archangel Gabriel, received the Word of God in her heart and in her body gave birth to the Son of God in our world. She conceived, gave birth to, and nourished Jesus; she presented him to God in the temple; and she shared in her divine Son's sufferings on the cross. Through her "yes" to God and her faith in the word of God, she occupies a unique place in salvation history, in the Church, and in the lives of believers. Therefore, we consider Mary our Mother and the Mother of the Church in the order of grace and faith.

The Church also presents to us exemplary models of faith and discipleship throughout Christian history in the "communion of saints." The Church does not "make" or "worship" the saints — rather, she recognizes the lives of saintly men and women through the ages as examples of faith, hope, and love worthy of our imitation as we journey in faith.

❖ God chose the Virgin Mary to be the Mother of his Son, Jesus Christ. Throughout the Old Testament, many other holy women prepared (foreshadowed) the role of Mary (*CCC* 488-489). All through the liturgical year, the Church celebrates feasts to honor the Blessed Mother of God.

❖ Mary is hailed by the Archangel Gabriel as she who is "full of grace." It was only fitting that the Holy Spirit prepared Mary to be capable of welcoming, in her heart and in her body, the inexpressible gift of God in Jesus Christ (*CCC* 721-726).

❖ The Virgin Mary "cooperated through free faith and obedience in human salvation." Her "yes" to God was uttered in the name of all human nature; by her obedience, she becomes the New Eve, mother of the living (*CCC* 511).

❖ Because of the unique and special role Mary plays in the plan of redemption, the Catholic tradition holds that she was enriched with gifts appropriate to such a role. From the first instant of her conception, she was totally preserved from the stain of Original Sin and remained pure from all personal sin throughout her life. This doctrine is celebrated in the feast of the Immaculate Conception, proclaimed on December 8, 1854, by Pope Pius IX (*CCC* 490-493).

❖ At her death Mary, preserved free from all stain of Original Sin, was taken up body and soul into heavenly glory. This doctrine of Mary's Assumption is an anticipation of the resurrection of all believers and is celebrated on the Feast of the Assumption, proclaimed in 1950 by Pope Pius XII (*CCC* 491, 966).

❖ Because of her unique role in bearing Jesus, the Son of God, into this world, the Church also holds that Mary "remained a virgin in conceiving and giving birth to her Son." Her virginity manifests God's absolute initiative and divine power in Mary, who conceives Jesus Christ "by the power of the Holy Spirit" (*CCC* 496-507).

❖ The "Hail Mary" is a prayer that echoes the unique role of Mary in the plan of our redemption. The Rosary is a meditative prayer that is a compendium, or summary, of the entire Gospel. By praying the Rosary, we join with Mary in contemplating the mysteries of Christ's life, death, and resurrection (*CCC* 971, 2673-2679).

❖ The "communion of saints" is the Church, broadly speaking. Specifically, the term "communion of saints" has two meanings: the community of all those who are baptized into Christ and who are now "pilgrims" on earth, the dead who are being purified to enter the presence of God, and the community of the saints — those holy men and women who are models of holiness, of faith, and love (*CCC* 946-962).

❖ The Church does not "make" saints. Rather, in canonizing a saintly man or woman, the Church publicly recognizes his or her exemplary cooperation with God's grace and his or her life of virtue, holiness, and love. The saints remind us of our heavenly goal and destiny in God. They are examples for all of us to follow on our faith journeys to God. All of us are called to holiness of life, to greater love and witness to Christ.

❖ In liturgical feasts and prayers, Catholics ask Mary, our Mother, and the saints to intercede to God on our behalf. The "communion of saints" reflects our belief in the power of intercessory prayer (*CCC* 2634-2636).

Read the Lesson of Faith — St. Juan Diego in the *United States Catholic Catechism for Adults*, pages 141-143.

Reflection: How does the Lesson of Faith illustrate the topic of this session?

APPLICATION TO CULTURE

Discussion

The following questions may be used to guide personal/group study and reflection along with the questions provided in the *United States Catholic Catechism for Adults,* page 147:

1. List the different ways in which Mary, Mother of God, is honored in the Catholic tradition.
2. How do you honor Mary, Mother of God?
3. Discuss challenges or common misconceptions concerning the role and place of Mary in the Christian life.
4. What does it mean to imitate the saints in the "call to holiness?"
5. Discuss how the examples of various American saints witness to Christian discipleship in this cultural context.

CONCLUSION

Read the Meditation and Prayer found in the *United States Catholic Catechism for Adults,* pages 148-149.

Make participants aware of the following suggestions for further reading and study:

Second Vatican Council, Dogmatic Constitution on the Church (*Lumen Gentium*), Chapter VIII, 52-69 (Our Lady).

Pope John Paul II, Mother of the Redeemer (*Redemptoris Mater*), March 1987.

———, The Rosary of the Virgin Mary (*Rosarium Virginis Mariae*), 2002.

Chapter 13

OUR ETERNAL DESTINY

INTRODUCTION

Prayer to the Holy Spirit, page 6

Choose one of the following Scripture readings:
- 1 Cor. 2:9-10
- Rom. 8:19-23
- 1 Tim. 2:4

Reflection Time

> **The *Catechism of the Catholic Church* and the Compendium**
>
> *CCC*: 988-1065
> Compendium:
> Questions 202-217

CATECHESIS

Read this Summary:

God desires that "all be saved and come to the knowledge of truth" (1 Tim. 2:4). God's desire for the salvation of every human person is the basis for our reflections on death, judgment, heaven, purgatory, hell, and eternal life with God. Only in light of God's unfailing offer of friendship and covenant love do we best understand Catholic beliefs about the "Last Things." In light of Jesus' victory over death in his resurrection we have the certain hope of our eternal union with God.

Created by God, each one of us was made with the capacity to be in relationship with God, in communion with God and with one another. Heaven is our ultimate destiny. During our earthly existence we grow in our relationship with God through prayer, reflection on God's word, the sacraments, and through our imitation of Jesus' example of love and service. Our ultimate destiny is eternal communion with God and with those united in Christ before God.

- ❖ The mystery of our future eternal communion with God is beyond human understanding or description in human language. The contemplation of God in his heavenly glory in the company of the saints and angels, called the "beatific vision," is the ultimate destiny of each one of us.
- ❖ The mystery of our eternal destiny with God and those united in Christ is beyond human understanding and description. Scripture describes heaven in images: life, light, peace, wedding feast, the Father's house, the heavenly Jerusalem, paradise (*CCC* 1027).
- ❖ Each person receives a "particular judgment" at the moment of death. Based on our love of God and neighbor, we are granted entrance to heaven into communion with God, to a period of purification, or to eternal separation from God (*CCC* 1021-1022).

❖ Those who die in God's grace and friendship enter into "heaven," which is the ultimate end and fulfillment of our deepest human longings for happiness. In heaven we enter into perfect communion with our Creator — what we were created for in the first place. Heaven is perfect existence with the Most Holy Trinity; it is communion of life and love with Christ and all those who believe in him and remained faithful to him (*CCC* 1023-1029).

❖ All who die in God's friendship but are still imperfect in their love for God are assured of eternal salvation; but after death they undergo purification, so as to be prepared to enter God's presence in the joy and light of heaven (*CCC* 1030).

❖ The Church gives the name *purgatory* to this final purification or cleansing of sins based on certain texts of Scripture that speak of a cleansing fire — 1 Cor. 3:15; 1 Pet. 1:7 (*CCC* 1031).

❖ The Catholic practice of praying for our deceased loved ones, particularly for those undergoing the purification of purgatory, is drawn from Scripture (2 Mac.12:36). From the beginning, the Church has honored the memory of the dead and offered prayers so that our departed loved ones through purification may attain the joy of heaven (*CCC* 1032).

❖ Through our own free choices, we can refuse to accept God's love and forgiveness. If we reject God's love by remaining in mortal sin (willful turning away from God), we separate ourselves from God forever. The state of "definitive self-exclusion from communion with God and the community of the blessed" is referred to as "hell" (*CCC* 1033). By choosing against God during our earthly life, we exclude ourselves from his eternal presence in heaven. "God predestines no one to go to hell" (*CCC* 1037).

❖ It is our responsibility to make use of our freedom and to pursue the path of daily conversion in view of our eternal life. Our profession of faith in God, the Father, the Son, and the Holy Spirit, culminates in the proclamation of the resurrection of the dead on the last day and in life everlasting (*CCC* 988).

❖ At the end of time, God's kingdom will come in fullness. "The 'Last Judgment,' or general judgment, will come when Christ returns in glory . . . we shall know the ultimate meaning of creation . . . and that God's love is stronger than death" (*CCC* 1038-1041).

Read the Lesson of Faith — St. Katharine Drexel in the *United States Catholic Catechism for Adults*, pages 151-152.

Reflection: How does the Lesson of Faith illustrate the topic of this session?

APPLICATION TO CULTURE

Discussion

The following questions may be used to guide personal/group study and reflection along with the questions provided in the *United States Catholic Catechism for Adults*, page 160:

1. How do Catholic teachings on eternal life help in understanding the mystery of human suffering and death?
2. Discuss reasons for Catholic beliefs about purgatory (*CCC* 1030-1037).
3. Discuss ways in which Catholic beliefs in eternal life differ from popular or contemporary understandings of life after death.
4. How would you explain to someone the Catholic practice of praying for the dead? (*CCC* 1032)
5. Why is the belief in the resurrection of our bodies important? (*CCC* 988-1004)

CONCLUSION

Read the Meditation and Prayer found in the *United States Catholic Catechism for Adults, page* 162.

Make participants aware of the following suggestions for further reading and study:

Lou Baldwin, *Saint Katharine Drexel: Apostle to the Oppressed*. The Catholic Standard and Times, 2000.

Second Vatican Council, Dogmatic Constitution on the Church *(Lumen Gentium)*, 48.

Pope John Paul II, On the Christian Meaning of Human Suffering (*Salvifici Doloris*), Apostolic Letter, February 11, 1984.

→ *Chapter 14* ←

THE CELEBRATION OF THE PASCHAL MYSTERY OF CHRIST

INTRODUCTION

Prayer to the Holy Spirit, page 6

Choose one of the following Scripture readings:
- Lk. 24:13-49 (Emmaus)
- Eph. 1:3-6
- Jn. 6:32; 20:21-23
- 1 Pet. 3:21

Reflection Time

> **The *Catechism of the Catholic Church* and the Compendium**
>
> *CCC*: 1076-1209
> Compendium:
> Questions 220-249

CATECHESIS

Read this Summary:

During his earthly ministry, Jesus preached and taught with authority and performed powerful healings and miracles through which he forgave sins and healed the wounds of sin. In the sacraments of the Church, Christ now **continues** the saving works he performed during his earthly life. In the sacraments, the Church offers to each of us the saving power of God in Jesus Christ for the healing of our whole person — spirit, soul, mind, and body — as we daily journey in faith with the community of believers.

❖ A sacrament may be defined as an "efficacious sign of grace, instituted by Christ and entrusted to the Church, by which divine life is dispensed to us. The visible rites by which the sacraments are celebrated signify and make present the graces proper to each sacrament. They bear fruit in those who receive them with the required dispositions" (*CCC* 1131).

❖ Jesus Christ now lives and acts in the Church through the sacraments, by which we are invited to participate in the mystery of his life, death, and resurrection (*CCC* 1076). We say the sacraments are *efficacious* because it is Christ himself at work in them: it is he who baptizes, he who forgives sins, he who acts in the sacraments in order to communicate the grace that each offers (*CCC* 1127-1129).

❖ The seven sacraments of the Church are the Sacraments of Initiation (Baptism, Confirmation, Eucharist), the Sacraments of Healing (Confession/Reconciliation, Anointing of the Sick), and the Sacraments of Service (Holy Orders, Matrimony). We believe that Christ Jesus instituted the seven sacraments.

❖ The sacraments of Baptism, Confirmation, and Eucharist are called the "Sacraments of Initiation" because they are steps toward union with Christ and the Church. The sacrament of Reconciliation (Confession) and the sacrament of Anointing of the Sick are called "Sacraments of Healing," as they heal soul, mind, and body. The "Sacraments of Service" are Holy Orders and Matrimony, given for the service of the Church and the world.

❖ In every sacramental celebration, we are led to deeper communion with God the Father, through Jesus Christ, in the power of the Holy Spirit. Each of the sacraments was instituted by Christ so that we may continue to participate in the divine life of grace and forgiveness he brings. Christ himself works in and through the visible rites and symbols of bread, wine, oil, and water taken from the world of creation. Christ is the guarantee of the sacramental graces that transform us into children of God.

❖ In the sacraments, the Church "celebrates above all the Paschal mystery by which Christ accomplished the work of our salvation. The mysteries of Christ's life are the foundations of what he would offer in the sacraments, through the ministers of the Church, for what was visible in our Savior has passed over into the sacraments" (*CCC* 1114-1116).

❖ The sacraments are "by the Church" and "for the Church." The Church is the primary sacrament, or sign, of Christ's saving actions. The sacraments are "for the Church" in that they "make" the Church, since they manifest the mystery of our communion with God (*CCC* 1117-1121).

❖ "The purpose of the sacraments is to sanctify us, to build up the Body of Christ, and finally, to give worship to God. They not only presuppose faith but they also nourish, strengthen, and express it. That is why they are called 'sacraments of faith'" (*CCC* 1122-1126).

❖ Sacraments express and signify the unity of faith within the Church. For that reason, they may only be received by Catholics.

❖ We celebrate the sacraments with signs and symbols (*CCC* 1145-1152), with words and actions (*CCC* 1153-1155), with singing and music (*CCC* 1156-1158) and — in liturgical time — Sundays and throughout the Liturgical Year (*CCC* 1163-1171).

Read the Lesson of Faith — Msgr. Martin Hellriegel in the *United States Catholic Catechism for Adults*, pages 165-166.

Reflection: How does the Lesson of Faith illustrate the topic of this session?

APPLICATION TO CULTURE

Discussion

The following questions may be used to guide personal/group study and reflection along with the questions provided in the *United States Catholic Catechism for Adults,* pages 176-177:

1. Based on the Catechism's definition of "sacrament," describe the purpose of the sacraments in the life of the Church and her members.
2. What does it mean to say that the sacraments continue the presence and saving work of Christ Jesus in the Church and in our lives?
3. What role do the sacraments play in your daily life, your spiritual life, and in prayer?

4. What does it mean to hold a "sacramental worldview?" How is a sacramental understanding of creation and humanity different from current popular culture?

5. Based on your reflection on the sacraments, how can you deepen your participation in the Eucharist?

CONCLUSION

Read the Meditation and Prayer found in the *United States Catholic Catechism for Adults,* page 178-179.

Make participants aware of the following suggestions for further reading and study

Joseph Cardinal Ratzinger, *The Spirit of the Liturgy.* Ignatius Press, 2000.

Second Vatican Council, Dogmatic Constitution on the Sacred Liturgy (*Sacrosanctum Concilium*), Chapter 1.

Pope John Paul II, On Catechesis in Our Time (*Catechesi Tradendae*), 23.

Pope Leo the Great, *Sermon 74*, 2.

St. Augustine, *The City of God,* Chapter 22.

Chapter 15
BAPTISM: BECOMING A CHRISTIAN

INTRODUCTION
Prayer to the Holy Spirit, page 6

Choose one of the following Scripture readings:
- Mt. 3:13-17
- Jn. 3:5
- Rom. 6:1-11

Reflection Time

The *Catechism of the Catholic Church* and the Compendium

CCC: 1210-1284
Compendium:
Questions 250-264

CATECHESIS
Read this Summary:

From the first moments of Christianity, new members were received into the Christian community through sacramental rites of initiation. The catechumenate, developed by early Christians during the first four centuries of the Church's existence, was an extensive spiritual, educational, and liturgical journey of initiation. The RCIA is a recent recovery of the ancient catechumenate that culminates in the celebration of the Sacraments of Initiation at the Easter Vigil.

The Sacraments of Baptism, Confirmation, and Eucharist were the sacramental rites through which new members — infants, children, and adults — were initiated into a new life of faith, hope, and love of Christ as members of his Body, the Church. Continuing this ancient tradition, today new members are welcomed into the Catholic Church through the Sacraments of Christian initiation.

The Sacraments of Christian Initiation (Baptism, Confirmation, and the Eucharist) are the spiritual foundations of every Christian life. Through the Sacraments of Initiation, the faithful are born anew by Baptism, strengthened by the Sacrament of Confirmation, and receive in the Eucharist the food of eternal life.

By means of the Sacraments of Christian Initiation, we are invited into communion with God in Jesus Christ, through the power of the Holy Spirit, to live a countercultural witness of faith. The Sacraments of Initiation fully incorporate us into the Body of Christ, the Church, and mark the beginning of a lifelong journey of faith.

❖ From the time of the apostles, initiation into the Christian community took place in several stages, through a journey of conversion. The *catechumenate*, developed to initiate new members into the Church, culminated at the Easter Vigil, when the catechumens received the sacraments of Initiation (*CCC* 1229-1233).

❖ Baptism, as the sacrament of faith, is the basis of the whole Christian life. Through Baptism, we are freed from the effects of Original Sin and reborn as adopted children of God through water and the Spirit; we become members of Christ's Body, the Church (*CCC* 1262-1271).

❖ Baptism is necessary for salvation, as affirmed by Jesus: "No one can enter the Kingdom of God without being begotten of water and the Spirit" (Jn. 3:5). Jesus also commands his disciples to proclaim the Gospel and baptize in the name of the Father, and of the Son, and of the Holy Spirit (Mt. 28:19-20).

❖ The essential rite of Baptism consists in immersing the candidate in water, or pouring water on his head, while pronouncing the invocation of the Most Holy Trinity: the Father, the Son, and the Holy Spirit. To baptize means to "immerse" or "plunge" into the water, symbolizing the catechumen's burial into Christ's death, from which he rises up by resurrection with him, as a "new creature" (*CCC* 1214). The sign of the cross, the baptismal water, the anointing with sacred chrism, the white garment, and the candle all signify the baptismal graces (1234-1245).

❖ "Incorporated into Christ by Baptism, we are configured to Christ. Baptism seals the Christian with an indelible spiritual mark of his belonging to Christ . . . Given once for all, Baptism cannot be repeated" (*CCC* 1272-1274)

❖ Our Baptism is a call to holiness, pursued in our vocations and in the daily ordinary circumstances of life (*CCC* 1270).

Read the Lesson of Faith — John Boyle O'Reilly in the *United States Catholic Catechism for Adults*, pages 181-182.

Reflection: How does the Lesson of Faith illustrate the topic of this session?

APPLICATION TO CULTURE
Discussion
The following questions may be used to guide personal/group study and reflection along with the questions provided in the *United States Catholic Catechism for Adults*, page 197:

1. What does the Sacrament of Baptism mean to you personally?
2. If Baptism is a "dying and rising with Christ," in the words of St. Paul (Rom. 6:3-4), how do you experience the grace of this sacrament daily?
3. How does Baptism strengthen you to be a better witness to Christ?
4. What role does faith play in Baptism? (*CCC* 1253-1255)
5. Discuss the meaning of the sacramental symbols and rite of Baptism (*CCC* 1234-1245).

CONCLUSION
Read the Meditation and Prayer found in the *United States Catholic Catechism for Adults,* pages 198-199.

Make participants aware of the following suggestions for further reading and study:
Second Vatican Council, Constitution on the Sacred Liturgy (*Sacrosanctum Concilium*), 64-65.
Introduction to the Rite of Baptism.
Introduction to the RCIA.

Chapter 16
CONFIRMATION: CONSECRATED FOR MISSION

INTRODUCTION
Prayer to the Holy Spirit, page 6

Choose one of the following Scripture readings:
- Acts 2:1-12
- Jn. 20:22
- Joel 3:1
- Acts 10:38

Reflection Time

CATECHESIS
Read this Summary:

The Holy Spirit, the third person of the Trinity, is the living presence of God in our lives promised by Jesus. The Holy Spirit strengthens our Christian witness so we may become the living reflections of Christ in the world. And so the Church prays, "Come, Holy Spirit, Creator blest, and in our souls take up thy rest. Come with thy grace and heavenly aid, to fill the hearts that thou hast made."

❖ The second sacrament of Initiation is Confirmation, the sacrament of the Holy Spirit that is intimately connected to Baptism and the Eucharist.

❖ The sacrament of Confirmation is a spiritual seal of the Holy Spirit that completes the sacramental graces received in Baptism. The effect of Confirmation is the outpouring of the Holy Spirit, as it was given to the apostles at Pentecost (*CCC* 1302-1305).

❖ Every baptized person receives the sacrament of Confirmation. Preparation for Confirmation invites us to deeper union with Jesus Christ and a greater reliance on the gifts and fruit of the Holy Spirit, who strengthens in us a sense of belonging to the Church and participation in her mission.

❖ "The reception of the sacrament of Confirmation is necessary for the completion of baptismal grace . . . By the sacrament of Confirmation the baptized are more perfectly bound to the Church and enriched with the special strength of the Holy Spirit" (*CCC* 1285).

> **The *Catechism of the Catholic Church* and the Compendium**
>
> *CCC*: 1285-1321
> Compendium:
> Questions 265-270

❖ Confirmation gives us a special strength of the Holy Spirit to profess our faith, by word and action, as true witnesses of Christ (*CCC* 1303). The Holy Spirit strengthens and guides us to live the Christian moral life and take our part in the mission of the Church.

❖ The Holy Spirit bestows seven gifts — Wisdom, Understanding, Knowledge, Fortitude, Counsel, Piety, and Fear of the Lord — to assist us in our Christian life and witness (*CCC* 1831). The fruits of the Spirit are Charity, Joy, Peace, Patience, Kindness, Goodness, Generosity, Gentleness, Faithfulness, Modesty, Self-Control, and Chastity (*CCC* 1832).

❖ The essential rite of Confirmation consists of anointing with chrism on the forehead, which is done by the laying on of hands, and through the words, "Be sealed with the gift of the Holy Spirit." The ordinary minister of Confirmation is the bishop (*CCC* 1299-1300; 1312-1314).

Read the Lesson of Faith — St. Frances Cabrini in the *United States Catholic Catechism for Adults*, pages 201-202.

Reflection: How does the Lesson of Faith illustrate the topic of this session?

APPLICATION TO CULTURE

Discussion

The following questions may be used to guide personal/group study and reflection along with the questions provided in the *United States Catholic Catechism for Adults*, pages 209-210:

1. Recall your experience of being confirmed. What does your sacramental confirmation mean to you today?
2. How does the Holy Spirit guide and strengthen our living out of the Christian moral life?
3. How are the gifts of the Holy Spirit made real in your daily life?
4. Which of the fruits of the Holy Spirit do you need to deepen and grow in?
5. Discuss the meaning of the sacramental symbols and rite of Confirmation (*CCC* 1297-1301).

CONCLUSION

Read the Meditation and Prayer found in the *United States Catholic Catechism for Adults*, page 211.

Make participants aware of the following suggestions for further reading and study:

Frances Parkinson Keyes, *Mother Cabrini: Missionary to the World*. Ignatius Press, 1997.

Pope John Paul II, Lord and Giver of Life (*Dominum et Vivificantem*), May 18, 1986.

Introduction to the Rite of Confirmation.

Chapter 17

EUCHARIST: SOURCE AND SUMMIT OF THE CHRISTIAN LIFE

———

INTRODUCTION
Prayer to the Holy Spirit, page 6

Choose one of the following Scripture readings:
- Ps.104
- Mt. 26:17-29
- Mk.14:12-25
- Lk. 22:14-20
- Jn.13:1-17, 34-35
- 1 Cor. 11:23-26
- Acts 2:42-46; 20:7

Reflection Time

CATECHESIS
Read this Summary:

The sacrament of the Eucharist, the "summary of our faith," completes sacramental Initiation. We believe that the Eucharist is the "source and summit of the Christian life" in that the Eucharist continues God's saving actions in Jesus Christ in every age of the Church. In our worship and union with Christ in the Eucharist, we grow in union with God in the power of the Holy Spirit. All the other sacraments are bound up with the Eucharist and are oriented toward it.

The word "Eucharist" comes from the Greek word *eucharistein,* meaning "thanksgiving." Jesus gave thanks at the Last Supper, at which he instituted the Eucharist, and then offered his sacrifice of praise and thanksgiving once for all on the Cross. In the Eucharistic memorial of his sacrifice on the Cross, he pours out graces of salvation on us who unite ourselves to him as sharers in his Body and Blood to form one single body.

At the Last Supper, Jesus instituted the Eucharistic sacrifice of his Body and Blood that perpetuates and continues his sacrifice on the Cross through the ages. He entrusts to the Church the memorial of his death and resurrection in this sacrament of love: a sign of unity, a bond of charity. When

> **The *Catechism of the Catholic Church* and the Compendium**
>
> *CCC:* 1322-1419
> Compendium:
> Questions 271-294

the Church celebrates the Eucharist, she commemorates Christ's Passover, and it is made present: the sacrifice Christ offered once for all on the cross remains ever present.

At the heart of the Eucharistic celebration are the bread and wine offered as the "work of human hands." By the words of Christ and the invocation of the Holy Spirit, the Eucharistic elements become Christ's Body and Blood. In the Eucharist, Christ gives us the very body he offered on the cross, the blood he "poured out for many for the forgiveness of our sins."

❖ The Eucharist completes sacramental Initiation. As the "repeatable sacrament of Initiation" it is the "source and the summit of the Christian life." All the other sacraments are oriented toward the Eucharist for it contains Christ himself whose presence heals, restores and forgives us (*CCC* 1322-1327).

❖ The word Eucharist means "thanksgiving." The *Catechism* lists several terms to describe the Eucharist: Lord's Supper, Breaking of Bread, Eucharistic assembly, memorial of the Lord's Passion and Resurrection, the Holy Sacrifice, the Holy and Divine Liturgy, the Most Blessed Sacrament, Holy Communion, and Holy Mass (*CCC* 1328-1332).

❖ Jesus instituted the Eucharist so that he might continue to abide with us and so that we might partake of the saving mystery of his passion, death and resurrection. Jesus' command to "do this in memory of me" is faithfully carried out by the Church from the very beginning to the end of time. The Eucharist is the center of the Church's life (*CCC* 1337-1345).

❖ The *memorial* of the Eucharist is not merely a recollection of past events but the proclamation of the mighty works wrought by God for us. . . . When the Church celebrates the Eucharist, she commemorates Christ's Passover and it is made present (*CCC* 1362-1364).

❖ The Eucharist is a sacrifice in that in it Christ gives us the very body which he gave up for us on the cross. The Eucharistic sacrifice *represents* the sacrifice of the cross. . . . The sacrifice of Christ and the sacrifice of the Eucharist are *one single sacrifice* (*CCC* 1365-1372).

❖ The Eucharist is sacrifice, thanksgiving, memorial, and presence (*CCC* 1356-1372).

❖ As the Paschal Banquet, the Eucharist unites us with Christ and with one another in the Body of Christ, the Church. The Eucharist makes the Church (*CCC* 1382-1405).

❖ We believe that in the Eucharist Christ is present "body and blood, soul and divinity . . . truly, really, and substantially." The consecration of bread and wine changes the whole substance of the bread into the substance of Christ's body and of the substance of the wine into the substance of his blood. This change is called "transubstantiation" (*CCC* 1373-1376). At every Eucharist, Christ offers himself for our nourishment and strength, to unite us with him and lead us to God in the power of the Holy Spirit.

❖ The Mass has two parts that together form "one single act of worship": the Liturgy of the Word and the Liturgy of the Eucharist (*CCC* 1346-1355).

Read the Lesson of Faith — Bl. Carlos Manuel Rodrigues in the *United States Catholic Catechism for Adults*, pages 213-214.

Reflection: How does the Lesson of Faith illustrate the topic of this session?

APPLICATION TO CULTURE

Discussion

The following questions may be used to guide personal/group study and reflection along with the questions provided in the *United States Catholic Catechism for Adults,* page 228:

1. Discuss the key events in the Passover meal of Jesus' Last Supper (Read Lk. 22:7-20; Mt. 26:17-29; Mk. 14:12-25).

2. What does it mean to "fully, consciously, and actively" participate in the Eucharist? What place does Eucharistic Adoration have in your spiritual life?

3. Share what you understand by Catholic teaching on the real presence of Christ in the Eucharist. Why is this teaching important?

4. What connections exist between the Eucharist and your daily life?

5. The Eucharist commits us to the needs of the poor (*CCC* 1397). How do you respond to Christ's presence in the sufferings and the needs of the poor?

CONCLUSION

Read the Meditation and Prayer found in the *United States Catholic Catechism for Adults,* pages 229-230.

Make participants aware of the following suggestions for further reading and study:

Joseph Cardinal Ratzinger, *Feast of Faith.* Ignatius Press, 1986.

————,*God is Near Us: The Eucharist.* The Heart of Life, 2003.

Second Vatican Council, Constitution on the Sacred Liturgy (*Sacrosanctum Concilium*), 1962.

Pope John Paul II, The Eucharist in its Relationship to the Church (*Ecclesia de Eucharistia*), 2003.

General Instruction of the Roman Missal.

Chapter 18

PENANCE AND RECONCILIATION:
GOD IS RICH IN MERCY

INTRODUCTION
Prayer to the Holy Spirit, page 6

Choose one of the following Scripture readings:
- Ps. 130
- Ps. 51
- Mk. 1:15; 2:1-12
- Lk. 7:48; 15:11-12
- Jn. 20:19, 22-23

Reflection Time

> **The *Catechism of the Catholic Church* and the Compendium**
>
> *CCC*: 1420-1498
> Compendium:
> Questions 295-312

CATECHESIS
Read this Summary:

Through the sacraments of Christian initiation, we receive the new life of Christ. But the weakness of our human nature and our inclination to sin continues to remain and affect our lives. The Church offers us the sacraments of healing to assist in the daily journey of conversion and reconciliation.

During his earthly ministry, Jesus forgave sins and healed those who were physically and spiritually broken. Those he forgave were healed, renewed in faith and restored to health of spirit, mind and body. The Church continues even today, in the power of the Holy Spirit, the healing work of Jesus Christ. This is the purpose of the two sacraments of healing: the sacrament of Penance and the sacrament of the Anointing of the Sick.

❖ When Jesus forgave sins, he also pointed to its effects: the reconciliation of sinners with God and with the community of believers. He gave the apostles his own power to forgive sins and reconcile sinners to God and to the Church (*CCC* 1443-1445).

❖ Only God forgives sins. Jesus willed that the Church be the sign and instrument of the forgiveness and reconciliation he won for us on the cross with his blood. He entrusted the power of absolution to the apostles and instituted the sacrament of Penance (Reconciliation), by which the baptized are offered new possibilities of conversion, forgiveness, and healing.

❖ Interior repentance is a radical reorientation of our whole life, a return to God with all of our heart, a turning away from sin and the resolution to change one's life with hope in God's mercy and grace (*CCC* 1430-1433).

❖ The sacrament comprises two essential elements: the actions of the penitent who undergoes conversion by the power of the Holy Spirit, namely contrition, confession, and penance; and God's reconciling action through the Church's mediation. Penance is a liturgical action (*CCC* 1480-1484).

❖ The "confessor" (the priest) is not the master of God's forgiveness but its servant. He forgives sins in the name of Jesus Christ, so that when he says, "I absolve you," the "I" is that of Christ. The "sacramental seal" of Penance means that every priest who hears confessions is bound to keep absolute secrecy regarding the sins confessed to him. What the penitent has made known to the priest remains "sealed" by the sacrament (*CCC* 1466-1467).

❖ The sacrament of Reconciliation restores us to God's grace and friendship, and reconciles us with the Church (*CCC* 1468-1470).

❖ Individual confession and absolution is the ordinary way for the faithful to be reconciled to God, the Church, and one another (*CCC* 1484).

❖ Every sin has personal and social consequences. Sin disrupts our union with God, weakens our ability to resist temptation, and hurts us and others. After receiving sacramental forgiveness, the necessity of healing the consequences of sin is called "temporal punishment." Prayer, fasting, almsgiving, and works of charity diminish the effects of sin. An "indulgence" is a full or partial remission of temporal punishment due to sin (*CCC* 1471-1479).

Read the Lesson of Faith — St. Augustine of Hippo in the *United States Catholic Catechism for Adults,* pages 233-234.

Reflection: How does the Lesson of Faith illustrate the topic of this session?

APPLICATION TO CULTURE

Discussion

The following questions may be used to guide personal/group study and reflection along with the questions provided in the *United States Catholic Catechism for Adults*, page 244:

1. Why do we need a sacrament of reconciliation after Baptism?
2. Discuss one example of a sinner turned saint, like St. Augustine. How does the saint exemplify God's unconditional and forgiving love?
3. Why confess sins to a priest? (*CCC* 1461-1467)
4. Discuss ways in which the Sacrament of Reconciliation is the response of God in Jesus Christ to the sinfulness of our human condition.
5. How can you partake more fully in the forgiving love of Christ made present in the Sacrament of Reconciliation?

CONCLUSION

Read the Meditation and Prayer found in the *United States Catholic Catechism for Adults,* pages 246-247.

Make participants aware of the following suggestions for further reading and study:

Pope John Paul II, Reconciliation and Penance (*Reconciliatio et Paenitentia*), 1984.

————, Rich in Mercy (*Dives in Misericordia*), 1980.

St. Augustine, *Confessions.*

Chapter 19

ANOINTING THE SICK AND THE DYING

INTRODUCTION

Prayer to the Holy Spirit, page 6

Choose one of the following Scripture readings:
- Lk. 6:19
- Ps. 23
- Mk. 1:41; 2:1-12; 3:10; 6:56
- Mt. 10:8; 25:36
- Jas. 5:14-15

Reflection Time

CATECHESIS

Read this Summary:

In his earthly ministry Jesus healed the whole person, body, mind, spirit, and soul. In the Gospels, we see Jesus healing the sick and forgiving sins. At times Jesus touched the ill and healed their sickness; at other times he spoke a healing word to them. Every Gospel account of Jesus' healing is accompanied by deepened faith, turning away from sin, and renewed commitment to Christian discipleship.

In the Church's sacrament of the Anointing of the Sick and the Dying, through the ministry of the priest, it is Jesus who continues to touch and heal the sick. Jesus healed as a visible sign of the coming of God's kingdom and of God's saving plan to conquer sin and death by the dying and rising of his Son, Jesus Christ.

We believe that the Church continues Jesus' healing ministry in and through the sacraments in general, and the sacrament of the Anointing of the Sick, in particular.

❖ The sacrament of the Anointing of the Sick strengthens the baptized when they experience grave illness or old age.

❖ The Anointing of the Sick "is not a sacrament for those only who are at the point of death. Hence as soon as anyone of the faithful begins to be in danger of death from sickness or old age, the fitting time to receive this sacrament has already arrived" (*CCC* 1514).

> ## The *Catechism of the Catholic Church* and the Compendium
>
> *CCC*: 1499-1532
> Compendium:
> Questions 313-320

❖ The celebration of the Anointing of the Sick consists in the anointing of the forehead and hands of the sick person accompanied with a liturgical prayer asking for special graces of strength, peace and courage.

❖ The primary effect of the sacrament of Anointing of the Sick is a spiritual healing by which the sick person receives the Holy Spirit's gift of peace and strength to deal with the difficulties that accompany serious illness or the frailty of old age. When the sacrament of Anointing is given, the hoped for effect is physical healing in accordance with God's will. Other effects of the sacrament are union with the passion of Christ; strength to endure the sufferings of illness or old age; the forgiveness of sins if the person was unable to receive the sacrament of Penance; and a preparation for the final journey from this life (*CCC* 1499-1532).

Read the Lesson of Faith — Joseph Cardinal Bernardin in the *United States Catholic Catechism for Adults,* pages 249-250.

Reflection: How does the Lesson of Faith illustrate the topic of this session?

APPLICATION TO CULTURE

Discussion

The following questions may be used to guide personal/group study and reflection along with the questions provided in the *United States Catholic Catechism for Adults,* page 257:

1. Discuss the ways in which the sacrament of Anointing the Sick continues the healing ministry of Jesus in the Gospels.
2. In what way does the sacrament of Anointing of the Sick make God's healing love real?
3. Recall examples of those who, through the grace of the sacrament of Anointing, witnessed to the peace and strength to bear the sufferings and limitations of sickness,
4. Discuss the various effects of the sacrament of Anointing.
5. Reflect on the rite of Anointing of the Sick and the meaning of each part of the ritual action (*CCC* 1519).

CONCLUSION

Read the Meditation and Prayer found in the *United States Catholic Catechism for Adults,* pages 258-259.

Make participants aware of the following suggestions for further reading and study:

Joseph Cardinal Bernardin, *The Journey to Peace: Reflections on Faith, Embracing Suffering, and Finding New Life.* Image Books, 2003.

Rite of Anointing of the Sick.

Chapter 20

HOLY ORDERS

INTRODUCTION
Prayer to the Holy Spirit, page 6

Choose one of the following Scripture readings:
- Mt.19:12
- Jn. 20:22-23
- Heb. 5:10; 6:20; 7:26; 10:14
- Acts 1:8; 2:4
- 1 Tim. 4:14
- 2 Tim. 1:6-7

Reflection Time

CATECHESIS
Read this Summary:

To serve God, the Church, and the faithful through the ministerial priesthood is a vocation, an invitation from the Lord that is a powerful countercultural witness of faith in Jesus Christ.

Through the Sacraments of Service — Holy Orders and Matrimony — those already baptized and confirmed receive particular vocations in service of God, the Church, and the human family. Those who receive Holy Orders are consecrated or set apart in the name of Jesus Christ to "feed the Church by the word and the grace of God."

❖ Holy Orders is the sacrament of "apostolic ministry" through which the mission that Christ entrusted to the apostles continues to be exercised in the Church. It includes three degrees: episcopate, presbyterate, and diaconate (*CCC* 1533-1600).

❖ In the service and person of the ordained minister, Christ, the high priest, is himself present to the Church. The priestly ministry reaches its summit in the priests' celebration of the Eucharist, the source and center of the Church's unity.

❖ All the baptized are a priestly people sharing in the priesthood of Christ. Based on this common priesthood, the sacrament of Holy Orders is a distinct participation in Christ's mission where the task of the ordained minister is to serve in the name and person of Christ the Head, *in persona Christi capitas,* in the midst of, and at the service of the community (*CCC* 1591).

❖ Only a baptized man may be ordained to the Sacrament of Holy Orders. This sacrament is a call from the Lord, not a right of any individual. Throughout his ministry, Jesus' attitude toward

The *Catechism of the Catholic Church* and the Compendium

CCC: 1536-1600
Compendium:
Questions 322-336

women was different from the culture of his day. However, Jesus chose twelve men to be his apostles and the foundation of the ministerial priesthood. The Church confers Holy Orders on baptized men following Christ, who chose men to be the twelve apostles and their successors. (*CCC* 1572-1580).

❖ The sacrament of Holy Orders is conferred on by the laying on of hands, followed by a prayer of consecration. Ordination imprints an indelible sacramental character (*CCC* 1572-1573; 1581-1584).

Read the Lesson of Faith — St. John Neumann in the *United States Catholic Catechism for Adults*, pages 261-262.

Reflection: How does the Lesson of Faith illustrate the topic of this session?

APPLICATION TO CULTURE

Discussion

The following questions may be used to guide personal/group study and reflection along with the questions provided in the *United States Catholic Catechism for Adults,* pages 272-273:

1. How is the ordained priesthood related to the common priesthood of all the baptized? (*CCC* 1142, 1547)
2. Discuss the reasons for Church teaching on reserving the priesthood to men (*CCC* 1577-1580).
3. List the qualities of a priest whose vocation is to imitate Christ's service to the community, the Church, and the world.
4. Discuss effective ways that priests and laity support each other for the common good of the Church and the world.
5. How might the laity support and encourage vocations to the priesthood and religious life?

CONCLUSION

Read the Meditation and Prayer found in the *United States Catholic Catechism for Adults,* pages 274-275.

Make participants aware of the following suggestions for further reading and study:

Joseph F. Chorpenning, *He Spared Himself in Nothing: Essays on the Life and Thought of St. John Nepomucene Neumann, C.S.S.R.* St. Joseph University Press, 2003.

Second Vatican Council, Decree on the Ministry and Life of Priests (*Presbyterorum Ordinis*), December 7, 1965.

Pope John Paul II, I Will Give You Shepherds (*Pastores Dabo Vobis*), 1992.

———, Consecrated Life (*Vita Consecrata*), 1996.

———, On Reserving Priestly Ordination to Men Alone (*Ordinatio Sacerdotalis*), 4.

Congregation for the Doctrine of the Faith, Declaration on the Admission of Women to the Ministerial Priesthood (*Inter Insignores*), 1976.

Chapter 21

THE SACRAMENT
OF MARRIAGE

INTRODUCTION
Prayer to the Holy Spirit, page 6

Choose one of the following Scripture readings:
- Gen.1:27-28; 2:18-25
- Song 8:6-7
- Hos. 2:21
- Mt.19:3-6
- Mk. 10:9
- Jn. 2:1-11
- 1 Cor. 7:10-11
- Eph. 5:25-32

Reflection Time

CATECHESIS
Read this Summary:

Sacred Scripture begins with the creation and the original unity of man and woman. In the last book of the Bible, we read of the "wedding feast of the Lamb" (Rev. 19:7, 9). The image of marriage is often used in Scripture to speak of God's covenant relationship with Israel and Christ's love for the Church.

In Genesis, God creates man and woman to live a shared life that is meant to reflect his love. Man and woman were created for each other (Gen. 2:18, 24) as equal in dignity and united in an unbreakable bond of love and fidelity.

The Christian understanding of marriage stands in contrast to popular attempts in society to change the definition and meaning of marriage. Efforts to make other kinds of unions equal to marriage contradict God's revealed law. The Catholic Church continues to be a wise voice teaching and witnessing to marriage as a covenant relationship that originates in God's plan of creation and salvation.

> **The *Catechism of the Catholic Church* and the Compendium**
>
> *CCC*: 1601-1666
> Compendium:
> Questions 337-350

❖ Sacramental marriage is a covenant between a man and a woman who form an intimate communion of life and love. Christ raised marriage to the dignity of a sacrament at Cana (Jn. 2:1-11) (*CCC* 1601, 1612-1617).

❖ God himself is the author of marriage. Since God created man and woman, their mutual love is an image of God's love for humanity. As a sacrament of the Church, marriage is not a purely human institution, but comes from the hand of the Creator (*CCC* 1603-1605).

❖ The spouses, as ministers of God's grace, mutually confer upon each other the Sacrament of Matrimony by expressing their consent before the Church within a Eucharistic liturgy. The Holy Spirit is the seal of their covenant and the source of their love and the strength to mutual fidelity (*CCC* 1621-1637).

❖ In his preaching and teaching, Jesus clearly taught the dignity and indissolubility of marriage (Mt. 19:3-6). In John's Gospel, Jesus' first miracle takes place at the wedding of Cana confirming the goodness of marriage as an efficacious sign of Christ's presence (*CCC* 1613).

❖ Matrimony signifies the union of Christ and the Church. Spouses are given the grace to love each other as Christ loved his Church. The grace of this sacrament perfects the love of spouses, strengthens their unity, and sanctifies them on the way to eternal life (*CCC* 1661).

❖ Unity, indissolubility, and openness to life are essential to the Catholic Sacrament of Marriage (1643-1654). The grace and presence of Christ in marriage protects the essential purposes of marriage: the good of the couple and the generation and education of children in the "domestic Church" of a Christian family (*CCC* 1660).

❖ The Sacrament of Marriage is a covenant, an agreement which exceeds the requirements of a contract. Marriage is a covenant between persons, a permanent union of persons capable of knowing and loving each other and God (*CCC* 1601).

Read the Lesson of Faith — St. Thomas More in the *United States Catholic Catechism for Adults*, pages 277-278.

Reflection: How does the Lesson of Faith illustrate the topic of this session?

APPLICATION TO CULTURE

Discussion

The following questions may be used to guide personal/group study and reflection along with the questions provided in the *United States Catholic Catechism for Adults,* pages 289-290:

1. Reflect on ways in which the Sacrament of Marriage as a covenant differs from the common cultural understanding of marriage as a contract.
2. Discuss how secular approaches to marriage impact the Christian family.
3. How can your family reflect more clearly its role as a "domestic Church?"
4. How can you support and offer hope to those in troubled marriages within your family, faith community, and society?
5. Does your family spend time together in prayer? When and how can you make prayer a regular dimension of your family life?

CONCLUSION

Read the Meditation and Prayer found in the *United States Catholic Catechism for Adults,* pages 291-292.

Make participants aware of the following suggestions for further reading and study:

James Monti, *The King's Good Servant but God's First: The Life and Writings of Saint Thomas More.* Ignatius Press, 1997.

Second Vatican Council, Pastoral Constitution on the Church in the Modern World (*Gaudium et Spes*), 47-52.

Pope John Paul II, The Christian Family (*Familiaris Consortio*), 1981.

———, Lay Members of Christ's Faithful (*Christifideles Laici*), 1988.

Chapter 22

SACRAMENTALS AND POPULAR DEVOTION

INTRODUCTION
Prayer to the Holy Spirit, page 6

Choose one of the following Scripture readings:
- Ps. 8
- Eph.1:3

Reflection Time

CATECHESIS
Read this Summary:

> **The *Catechism of the Catholic Church* and the Compendium**
>
> *CCC*: 1667-1679
> Compendium:
> Questions 351-353

Sacramentals are sacred signs instituted by the Church that mediate spiritual effects such as blessings, protection, and peace through the Church. They bear resemblance to the sacraments and signify effects, particularly spiritual effects, obtained through the mediation of the Church (*CCC* 1667).

The Church instituted sacramentals so that the faithful may be better disposed to participate fully in the sacraments and receive divine blessings and protection. The use of sacramentals in daily life is often accompanied by a prayer, usually with a ritual gesture such as the Sign of the Cross or sprinkling of holy water.

- ❖ Sacramentals include blessings, ritual actions such as processions, prayers and devotions such as the Rosary, and objects, such as medals of saints. They bear resemblance to the sacraments and signify effects — particularly spiritual effects — obtained through the mediation of the Church (*CCC* 1667).

- ❖ Making the Sign of the Cross at the beginning and end of each day, praying morning and evening prayers, and praying before and after a meal are some of the daily ways in which we invoke and experience God's blessings on our lives.

- ❖ Among the sacramentals, blessings hold a major place. There are blessings for persons, meals, objects, places, and important occasions such as graduations, welcomes, and farewells. All blessings focus on praising God for his manifold gifts. Most blessings invoke the Holy Trinity, expressed in the Sign of the Cross, together with the sprinkling of holy water.

- ❖ Expressions of piety and devotion extend the liturgical life of the Church but do not replace it. Catholic devotions and prayers of piety are all directed to foster more active, full, and conscious participation in the Eucharist (*CCC* 1675).

- ❖ Popular prayers and devotions are the means by which we permeate everyday life with prayer. In the Catholic tradition, examples of popular devotions include pilgrimages, novenas, processions in honor of Mary and/or the saints, the Rosary, the Angelus, the Stations of the Cross, veneration of relics, and the use of sacramentals. Properly used, such popular devotional practices extend the sacramental graces of the Eucharist into daily life, not replace it.

❖ The Rosary is a prayer based on Scripture. It is the Gospel turned into meditative prayer. The mysteries of the Rosary center on the events of Christ's life, death, and resurrection. The repetition of the Hail Mary, taken from the words of the Archangel Gabriel in Luke's Gospel (Lk. 1:29 and 1:42), are meant to lead us into a meditative and contemplative praying of the Gospel.

❖ Sacred images — icons, statues and paintings of saints, and stained glass — are all meant to move the faithful to contemplation on the Word of God and on the mysteries of Christ through visible images of beauty. Just as the invisible God was made visible in Jesus Christ, Christian images make visible invisible mysteries of faith (*CCC* 1159-1162, 2500-2503).

Read the Lesson of Faith — Father Patrick Peyton, CSC, in the *United States Catholic Catechism for Adults*, pages 293-295.

Reflection: How does the Lesson of Faith illustrate the topic of this session?

APPLICATION TO CULTURE

Discussion

The following questions may be used to guide personal/group study and reflection along with the questions provided in the *United States Catholic Catechism for Adults,* page 301:

1. Name one Catholic devotion in which you participate and share how it affects your faith life. Does it lead you to greater love of the Eucharist?
2. How would you explain the Catholic tradition of "sacramentals" to someone who has never experienced them?
3. How are prayers of blessing of homes, persons, and objects beneficial to the spiritual life?
4. Discuss benefits of praying the Rosary or the Stations of the Cross.
5. What is the value of sacred and religious art — crucifixes, statues, and holy images — in churches and special places in Catholic homes?

CONCLUSION

Read the Meditation and Prayer found in the *United States Catholic Catechism for Adults,* pages 302-303.

Make participants aware of the following suggestions for further reading and study:

Michael Dubruiel and Amy Welborn, *Praying the Rosary with the Joyous, Luminous, Sorrowful, and Glorious Mysteries*. Our Sunday Visitor, 2004.

All for her: The Autobiography of Father Patrick Peyton. Family Theater Publications, 1973.

Patrick Peyton, *Father Peyton's Rosary Prayer Book: The Family That Prays Together Stays Together*. Ignatius Press, 2003.

Pope John Paul II, On the Most Holy Rosary (*Rosarium Virginis Mariae*), 2002.

United States Conference of Catholic Bishops, *Popular Devotional Practices: Basic Questions and Answers*, November 2003.

Vatican Congregation for Divine Worship and the Discipline of the Sacraments, *Directory on Popular Piety and the Liturgy*, December 2001.

PART III — MORAL LIFE

⟶ *Chapter 23* ⟵

LIFE IN CHRIST, PART ONE

INTRODUCTION
Prayer to the Holy Spirit, page 6

Choose one of the following Scripture readings:
- Mt. 5:3-12; 9:17; 19:16-22; 22:37-39
- Rom. 2:1:32; 2:14-16; 6:11; 12:15
- 1 Cor. 12-13
- Col. 3-4
- Eph. 4-5
- Gal. 5:22-23

> **The *Catechism of the Catholic Church* and the Compendium**
>
> *CCC*: 1691-2082
> Compendium:
> Questions 357-441

Reflection Time

CATECHESIS
Read this Summary:

To be human is to be faced with moral choices: "to do what is good and avoid evil." The sacraments of Initiation, Healing, and Service strengthen us with the wisdom and capacity to choose what is good and avoid evil. Our free will and intellect are manifestations of our being made in the image of God.

Living according to the Ten Commandments bears witness to our dignity as human beings made in the image and likeness of God. The Commandments are not impositions on our freedom nor are they a list of rules and laws, or dos and don'ts. Rather the Ten Commandments are a divine invitation to grow in authentic freedom and shape our lives in accordance with God's plan for humanity. By contrast, popular culture exalts individual morality, moral relativism, and autonomy above tradition and community.

"Teacher, what good deed must I do to have eternal life?" is the question posed to Jesus in Matthew's Gospel. Jesus' answer is our challenge as well: "if you would enter life, keep the commandments" (Mt.19:17). In striving to live the Ten Commandments, we respond to the human desire for happiness that God has placed in our hearts as we are confronted with decisive choices. The Ten Commandments teach us the love of God above all things and loving service of our neighbors.

The Ten Commandments take on their full meaning within God's covenant of love, mercy, and forgiveness. They express the implications of belonging to God and the Christian community of the

Church. Living a Christian moral life is our response to God's love and our cooperation with the plan of God in human history.

❖ Incorporated into Christ by baptism, a Christian is "dead to sin and alive to God in Jesus Christ" (Rom. 6:11). To follow Christ and be united with him is to strive to be "imitators of God as beloved children, and to walk in love" by conforming our thoughts, words, and actions to God's commands (*CCC* 1694-1696).

❖ Endowed with a spiritual soul, with intellect and free will we are ordered to God and destined for eternal beatitude or happiness. Human freedom and the power of reason or the intellect are manifestations of the divine image (*CCC* 1701-1715).

❖ The Beatitudes (Mt. 5:3-12) are at the heart of Jesus' preaching. They respond to our natural human desire for happiness. God has placed this desire in each human heart in order to draw us to God, who alone can perfectly fulfill it (*CCC* 1716-1728).

❖ Human freedom is the power, rooted in reason and will, to act or not to act based on one's responsibility. True human freedom is to act at the service of what is good and just (*CCC* 1731). Freedom makes us moral subjects such that actions chosen freely through a judgment of conscience can be morally evaluated as good or evil (*CCC* 1749).

❖ The right to exercise our freedom in moral and religious matters is an inalienable requirement of the dignity of the human person. Authentic freedom is not freedom *from* personal responsibility, but freedom *for* love of God and neighbor (*CCC* 1738).

❖ Freedom as the power to act or not to act — especially in religious and moral matters — is an inalienable aspect of the dignity of human persons. Freedom is perfected when it is directed to God. Freedom is not be confused with license, the putative right to say or do anything (*CCC* 1744, 1747).

❖ Conscience is a law inscribed by God on the human heart that calls us to love and to choose good and avoid evil. Conscience is a judgment of reason whereby the human person recognizes the moral quality of a concrete act and assumes responsibility for it (*CCC* 1776-1782).

❖ A well-formed conscience judges according to reason, the will of God in the Word of God, and the moral teachings of the Church. The education of conscience is a lifelong task guided by the light of the Word of God, prayer, the gifts of the Holy Spirit, the witness and advice of others, and the teachings of the Church (*CCC* 1783-1785).

❖ Virtue is a habitual and firm disposition to do good. The human virtues are stable dispositions of the intellect and will that govern our actions, order our passions and desires, and guide our conduct, in accordance with reason and faith. The four cardinal virtues are prudence, justice, fortitude, and temperance. The three theological virtues are faith, hope, and charity (*CCC* 1833, 1834, 1841).

❖ The Ten Commandments state what is required in the love of God and neighbor. The first three commands concern love and fidelity to God, while the other seven speak of love and forgiveness of neighbor as an expression of love of God (*CCC* 2067).

❖ What God commands, he makes possible through divine grace. When we believe in Jesus Christ, participate in the sacraments, and persevere in daily prayer and reflection on God's word, we draw on divine grace and the strength to live according to the commandments (*CCC* 2074).

❖ Grace is the help God gives us to live our vocation as adopted children of God. Grace introduces us into the intimacy of the Trinitarian life, wherein God's initiative precedes, prepares, and elicits our free response. Grace responds to the deepest yearnings of human freedom (*CCC* 2021-2022).

❖ *Sanctifying grace* is a habitual gift, a stable and supernatural inclination to do good. *Habitual grace*, the permanent disposition to live and act in keeping with God's law, is distinguished from *actual graces,* which are God's concrete interventions in the course of our sanctification (*CCC* 2000).

❖ Justification is both the work of the Holy Spirit — in forgiving our sins —and our acceptance of God's grace, through which we are enabled to live by God's law.

Read the Lesson of Faith — Jesus the Teacher in the *United States Catholic Catechism for Adults*, pages 307-309.

Reflection: How does the Lesson of Faith illustrate the topic of this session?

APPLICATION TO CULTURE

Discussion

The following questions may be used to guide personal/group study and reflection along with the questions provided in the *United States Catholic Catechism for Adults,* page 319:

1. How is your striving to live by the Ten Commandments an expression of your love for God and your neighbor?
2. How do the Beatitudes (Mt. 5:3-12) reveal the goal of human existence? In what way do the Beatitudes respond to the desire for happiness placed in us by God?
3. Discuss steps you can take to form your conscience in light of the fullness of Church teachings. Reflect on the ways in which conscience formation runs counter to the individualistic morality of our age.
4. Reflect on the obstacles, challenges, and difficulties you face in following the Commandments. How can you rely more on divine wisdom and strength when faced with moral decisions?
5. What particular virtue would you like to grow in? What vice(s) do you need to overcome? How might you strengthen virtues in your daily life?

CONCLUSION

Read the Meditation and Prayer found in the *United States Catholic Catechism for Adults,* page 321.

Make participants aware of the following suggestions for further reading and study:

Second Vatican Council, Pastoral Constitution on the Church in the Modern World (*Gaudium et Spes*), 7, 16, 30.

Pope John Paul II, The Splendor of Truth (*Veritatis Splendor*), 1993.

Chapter 24

LIFE IN CHRIST, PART TWO

INTRODUCTION
Prayer to the Holy Spirit, page 6

Choose one of the following Scripture readings:
- Ps. 139
- Jer. 1:5
- Ex. 20:13
- Deut. 5:17
- Mt. 5:43-44; 6:33; 25:40
- Gal. 3:28
- Eph. 2:14

Reflection Time

> ### The *Catechism of the Catholic Church* and the Compendium
>
> *CCC:* 1691-2082
> Compendium:
> Questions 357-441

CATECHESIS
Read this Summary:

Respect for the dignity of each human person involves respect for the rights that flow from that dignity. Created in the image and likeness of God (Gen. 1:26), all human beings are endowed with rational souls; all have the same human nature and same origin and destiny. Redeemed by Jesus Christ, all are invited to enjoy equal dignity as children of God.

The Church affirms the sacredness and dignity of the life of every human person. The Church teaches that we are human beings from the moment of conception to natural death. Our origin and destiny is in God, our Creator.

Social justice can become a reality only when the transcendent dignity of each person is respected, safeguarded, and promoted. During the past century, the Church has articulated a systematic body of moral teachings on social issues. This body of social teaching constitutes an essential part of Christian moral life, based on the Gospel demands of love and justice.

In Catholic social teaching, the Church develops principles to evaluate social structures that serve both individuals and the common good. The Church's moral and spiritual guidelines are offered to us as a guide for personal morality and a means to evaluate just or unjust social structures.

❖ The equality of human beings rests essentially on their dignity as persons and the rights that flow from that dignity (*CCC* 1934-1938). Natural law is our rational apprehension of the created moral order, based on the fact that we are created in God's image. It expresses our human dignity.

❖ Society ensures social justice when it provides the conditions that allow individuals or groups to obtain what is their due, according to their nature and their vocation. Social justice can be obtained only in respecting the transcendent dignity of every human person. The person represents the ultimate end of society (*CCC* 1929-1933).

❖ Social sin is that "sin that makes men accomplices of one another and causes concupiscence, violence, and injustice to reign among them. Sins give rise to social situations and institutions contrary to the divine goodness. 'Structures of sin' are the expression and effect of personal sins. They lead their victims to do evil in their turn" (*CCC* 1869).

❖ Socioeconomic problems may be resolved with the help of all forms of solidarity: solidarity among the poor; between rich and poor; among workers; between employers and workers; and among nations and peoples. Solidarity, or "social charity," is a direct demand of the Gospel. The Christian virtue of solidarity involves the sharing of both material and spiritual goods (*CCC* 1939-1942).

❖ When Jesus proclaims the coming of God's kingdom, he speaks of salvation from sin and injustice (Lk. 4:14-21). Throughout his ministry, Jesus speaks against the unjust practices of the Pharisees and tax collectors. The Beatitudes (Mt. 5:3-12), the parables of the Good Samaritan (Lk.10:29-37), and the Rich Man and Lazarus (Lk.16:19-31) show Jesus' concern and compassion for the poor and the outcast. By healing the sick, the abandoned, and the poor, Jesus teaches us the value of each human life.

❖ From its conception, the child has the right to life. Direct abortion and intentional euthanasia are grave contradictions of the dignity of human life and the respect due to God, our Creator. Because a human being should be treated as a person from conception, the human embryo must be defended in its integrity, cared for, and healed like every other human being (*CCC* 2258-2330).

Read the Lesson of Faith — Cesar Chavez in the *United States Catholic Catechism for Adults*, pages 323-324.

Reflection: How does the Lesson of Faith illustrate the topic of this session?

APPLICATION TO CULTURE

Discussion

The following questions may be used to guide personal/group study and reflection along with the questions provided in the *United States Catholic Catechism for Adults,* page 335:

1. The Christian moral life is based on God's loving plan of salvation, revealed in the Scriptures. How do you strive to live the Christian moral life as an expression of love for God?
2. Living the Catholic faith invites the faithful assent of every baptized Catholic to Church teachings on faith and morals. How do you strive to understand and live by the Church's moral teachings?
3. Identify ways you can seek God's grace so as to live by the Commandments.
4. How do you concretely express your solidarity with the poor in your community, city, country, and world?

5. How would you explain the Church's teaching that the "right to life" and the dignity of every human person are the most fundamental principles of Catholic social justice?

CONCLUSION

Read the Meditation and Prayer found in the *United States Catholic Catechism for Adults,* pages 337-338.

Make participants aware of the following suggestions for further reading and study:

Frederick John Dalton, *The Moral Vision of Cesar Chavez.* Orbis, 2003.

Pope Leo XIII, On the Condition of Labor (*Rerum Novarum*), 1891.

Pope Pius XI, On the Fortieth Anniversary of *Rerum Novarum* (*Quadragesimo Anno*), 1931.

Pope John XXIII, Peace on Earth (*Pacem in Terris*), 1963.

Pope John Paul II, On the Value and Inviolability of Human Life (*Evangelium Vitae*), 1995.

———, *Centesimus Annus*, 1991.

Second Vatican Council, Pastoral Constitution on the Church in the Modern World (*Gaudium et Spes*), 63-90.

Chapter 25

THE FIRST COMMANDMENT: BELIEVE IN THE ONE TRIUNE GOD

INTRODUCTION
Prayer to the Holy Spirit, page 6

Choose one of the following Scripture readings:
- Ps. 77
- Deut. 5:6; 6:5

Reflection Time

CATECHESIS
Read this Summary:

God has first loved the world; the first of the Ten Commandments speaks of our response to God's love. To believe in the One Triune God with our whole heart, mind, body, and soul is our human response to God's unconditional love. The First Commandment invites us to believe in the true God, to hope in him, and to love him fully with our hearts, minds, and wills. This commandment moves us to praise, worship, and adoration of God alone, because God alone is holy and worthy of our praise.

The First Commandment points to the Christian belief in the One Triune God — neither as an abstraction nor a philosophical or psychological entity, but as a personal reality of faith. Belief in God is an invitation to entrust oneself to a loving and personal God who is Father, Son, and Holy Spirit. In this way the first Commandment calls forth the human response of faith, hope, and love.

Idolatry, or the worship of false gods, is prohibited by the First Commandment. The people of Israel were commanded not to make or worship graven images. The Incarnation of God in Jesus Christ provided the basis for Christian images of Christ, Mary, the saints, and the events and figures of the Bible. The veneration and honor given to sacred images of Mary and the saints is to be distinguished from the adoration and worship that belongs to God alone.

❖ "I am the LORD your God . . . You shall have no other gods before me . . . You shall love the LORD your God with all your heart, and with all your soul, and with all your might" (Deut. 5:6, 6:5).

> **The *Catechism of the Catholic Church* and the Compendium**
>
> *CCC*: 2083-2141
> Compendium:
> Questions 442-446

❖ The First Commandments invite us to the practice of the Theological Virtues of faith, hope, and love. The virtue of faith is our personal response to God's self revelation of love, holiness, and transcendent beauty. Hope is the confidence that God abides with us on the journey of life. Love of God is our response to God's unconditional love for us. Jesus made love of God the first of the two greatest commandments (Mt. 22:37) (*CCC* 1812-1829).

❖ We believe in One Triune God as an article of Christian faith. We adore God because he alone is God and worthy of our praise and adoration. Idolatry is a distortion of man's innate virtue of religion. The First Commandment to worship God alone integrates man and saves him from an endless disintegration (*CCC* 2114).

❖ The First Commandment forbids idolatry; that is, the false worship of a creature or an object. Contemporary forms of idolatry give absolute value and primacy to created things rather than to the Creator. Greed and materialism are among the common forms of idolatry today. Atheism, radical secularism, and agnosticism are also forms of rejecting the First Commandment.

❖ In striving to live by the First Commandment, we give the assent of mind and will to God alone, all that the Church as teacher and mother offers, and all that is presented to us by the Church in her ordinary and universal Magisterium.

Read the Lesson of Faith — Catherine de Hueck Doherty in the *United States Catholic Catechism for Adults*, pages 339-341.

Reflection: How does the Lesson of Faith illustrate the topic of this session?

APPLICATION TO CULTURE

Discussion

The following questions may be used to guide personal/group study and reflection along with the questions provided in the *United States Catholic Catechism for Adults*, page 347:

1. How are Christian beliefs about God different from common cultural notions of God's nature and existence?
2. How do you concretely live out the theological virtues of faith, hope, and love on a daily basis?
3. How can you grow in your response to the first Commandment?
4. List some of the distractions offered by popular culture that obscure the revelation of God in our world.
5. How have you experienced God's love and power in your life?

CONCLUSION

Read the Meditation and Prayer found in the *United States Catholic Catechism for Adults*, pages 348-349.

Make participants aware of the following suggestions for further reading and study:

Lorene Hanley Duquin, *They Called Her the Baroness: The Life of Catherine De Hueck Doherty.* Alba House, 1996.

Second Vatican Council, Pastoral Constitution on the Church in the Modern World (*Gaudium et Spes*), 19-21, 53-62.

Pope John Paul II, The Splendor of the Truth (*Veritatis Splendor*), 1993.

✦ *Chapter 26* ✦

THE SECOND COMMANDMENT: REVERENCE GOD'S NAME

—◆◆◆—

INTRODUCTION
Prayer to the Holy Spirit, page 6

Choose one of the following Scripture readings:
- Ps. 103:1
- Ex. 3:14
- Is. 43:1
- Jn. 8:58
- Acts 4:12
- Jas. 3:2-12
- Phil. 2:9-10

> **The *Catechism of the Catholic Church* and the Compendium**
>
> *CCC*: 2142-2167
> Compendium:
> Questions 447-449

Reflection Time

CATECHESIS
Read this Summary:

The Second Commandment invites us to reverence the holy name of God. Reverence for the name of God belongs to the virtue of religion as it is expressed in our speech about sacred matters.

God revealed his name to Moses when he said to him, "I AM who am" (Ex. 3:14). Out of reverence for the name of God, the Israelites used the name *Adonai,* which means *Lord.* In John's Gospel, Jesus applies to himself the name "I AM" (Jn. 8:58) and reveals his divine identity as the Son of God.

A name expresses and conveys the identity and reality of a person — the origins and life story of a person. That is why we expect that our names be treated with respect and reverence. In the same way, the name of God deserves the highest honor and respect.

In the Eucharist, we praise God's holy name when we recite or sing the "Holy, Holy, Holy" and in the words of the first petition of the Our Father, that is, "Hallowed be thy name." In Baptism, we are incorporated into the Church "in the name of the Father, and of the Son, and of the Holy Spirit." To be baptized in God's name is to be sanctified by God.

❖ The Second Commandment invites us to respect God's name. Doing so belongs to the virtue of religion as it applies to our daily speech and reverence for the name of God (*CCC* 2142).

❖ God calls each of us by name out of love and mercy. In calling out to God, we too should give due reverence and respect to God's name. In praying the Divine Praises, we reverence the name of God the Father, the Son, and the Holy Spirit, the Blessed Virgin Mary, Joseph, and the angels and saints.

❖ The Second Commandment prohibits the wrong use of the name of God in speech or written words. Blasphemy is an inward or outward utterance against God in words of hatred, reproach, or defiance. Blasphemy wrongly uses the name of God and of Jesus Christ, of the Blessed Virgin Mary, and the saints to disrespect God's holy name (*CCC* 2148, 2162). Christians are forbidden to use God's name to witness a perjury or false oath.

❖ At our Baptism, we receive a name in the Church. It is common practice to receive the name of a saint or other Christian model as an example and reminder of our call to holiness. Patron saints intercede on our behalf (*CCC* 2165).

Read the Lesson of Faith — Job in the *United States Catholic Catechism for Adults*, pages 351-353.

Reflection: How does the Lesson of Faith illustrate the topic of this session?

APPLICATION TO CULTURE

Discussion

The following questions may be used to guide personal/group study and reflection along with the questions provided in the *United States Catholic Catechism for Adults,* pages 357-358:

1. How do you strive to live by the Second Commandment?
2. How would you explain the wrong use of God's name when you hear or see God's name being disrespected?
3. How can you help young people become aware of the blasphemy common in television, popular music, and films?
4. Share strategies to addressing the problem of coarse language and blasphemy when it occurs in your hearing or sight.
5. How can you deepen your reliance on the Holy Spirit to guard your speech?

CONCLUSION

Read the Meditation and Prayer found in the *United States Catholic Catechism for Adults,* pages 358-359.

Make participants aware of the following suggestions for further reading and study:

The Divine Praises.

St. Ignatius of Loyola, *Spiritual Exercises,* 38.

✥ Chapter 27 ✥

THE THIRD COMMANDMENT: LOVE THE LORD'S DAY

———◆◆◆———

INTRODUCTION
Prayer to the Holy Spirit, page 6

Choose one of the following Scripture readings:
- Ex. 20:8-11
- Deut. 5:12
- Is. 58:14

Reflection Time

CATECHESIS
Read this Summary:

> **The *Catechism of the Catholic Church* and the Compendium**
>
> *CCC:* 2168-2195
> Compendium:
> Questions 450-454

In Genesis, God rests on the seventh day after his work of creating the world. God builds into human nature a balanced rhythm of work and rest, whereby we are refreshed from our work and return our hearts and minds to worship God.

The Third Commandment exhorts us to keep holy the Sabbath day. The biblical basis for the Third Commandment is the Lord's command to Israel: "Observe the Sabbath day, to keep it holy, as the Lord your God commanded you. Six days you shall labor and do all your work; but the seventh day is a Sabbath to the LORD your God" (Deut. 5:12-13).

❖ For Christians, the observance of the Sabbath is transferred to Sunday, the day that Jesus rose from the dead. In the Christian liturgical calendar, Sunday extends the celebration of Easter, as it makes present the new creation of the risen Christ. It recalls the first creation and the saving work of the risen Jesus in the new creation.

❖ On Sunday, Catholics keep the Sabbath holy by participating in the Eucharist and by prayerful reflection on God's word. Participation in the Sunday Eucharist renews the bonds of faith and unity.

❖ Keeping the Lord's Day holy is a way of putting all human activity into perspective with God. Sunday rest creates a time and space when we once again recognize the wonder and beauty of God's creation. The Lord's Day is also an important time for families to be together.

❖ The hectic pace of modern life and the worldview of a "consumer" society conspire to keep us focused on productivity and material wealth. The relentless activity that marks a consumerist society causes many people not to rest or worship God on Sunday. Making the celebration of the Lord's Day a priority is an expression of our love for God and a means to be renewed in the light of God's love.

Read the Lesson of Faith — Fr. Demetrius Gallitzin and Fr. James Fitton in the *United States Catholic Catechism for Adults*, pages 361-363.

Reflection: How does the Lesson of Faith illustrate the topic of this session?

APPLICATION TO CULTURE

Discussion

The following questions may be used to guide personal/group study and reflection along with the questions provided in the *United States Catholic Catechism for Adults,* page 369:

1. Describe how you spend a typical Sunday. Is Sunday a time of worship, rest, and relaxation for you?
2. How does your participation in the Sunday Eucharist prepare and renew you for the daily activities of the rest of the week?
3. Discuss ways in which consumerism and secularism undermine the Christian practice of keeping the Lord's Day holy.

CONCLUSION

Read the Meditation and Prayer found in the *United States Catholic Catechism for Adults*, pages 370-371.

Make participants aware of the following suggestions for further reading and study:

Second Vatican Council, Dogmatic Constitution on the Sacred Liturgy (*Sacrosanctum Concilium*), 48.

Pope John Paul II, Keeping The Lord's Day Holy (*Dies Domini*), 1998.

Chapter 28

THE FOURTH COMMANDMENT: STRENGTHEN YOUR FAMILY

INTRODUCTION

Prayer to the Holy Spirit, page 6

Choose one of the following Scripture readings:
- Ps. 78:1-7
- Sir. 3; 7:27-28
- Prov. 23:22
- Lk. 2:51
- Jn. 2:1-11

Reflection Time

CATECHESIS

Read this Summary:

The Fourth Commandment, "Honor your father and your mother," focuses on family life in all its dimensions — the duties and responsibilities of parents and children.

The Sacrament of Marriage creates and sustains the Christian family so that it truly reflects the Gospel lived out in the ordinary daily circumstances of life. The Holy Trinity as a loving communion of divine persons — Father, Son and Holy Spirit — and the Holy Family of Nazareth with Jesus, Mary, and Joseph — are models for every Christian family.

We take up the challenge to strengthen our families within a culture that often undermines the values of fidelity, self-sacrifice, and faith. The widespread values of secular society deny the role of the family as the basic nucleus of society and challenge Christians to greater commitment to this commandment.

The Church holds that "a man and a woman united in marriage, together with their children, form a family" (*CCC* 2202). Over and above this basic nucleus of society, other family relationships have developed such as single-parent families, blended families, and extended families that unite generations of family members. All Christian families are called to be a "domestic Church," wherein all members grow in faith, hope, and love.

The *Catechism of the Catholic Church* and the Compendium

CCC: 2196-2257
Compendium:
Questions 455-465

❖ Marriage and family are ordered to the good of the spouses . . . to the procreation and education of children (*CCC* 2249).

❖ Parents have the primary responsibility for the education in the faith of their children, of growth in prayer and in virtue. Parents provide as far as they are able for the physical and spiritual needs of their children (*CCC* 2252).

❖ Children owe to parents respect, gratitude, just obedience, and support and care. Such respect fosters and strengthens the bonds and harmony in family life (*CCC* 2251).

❖ This commandment also includes the duty of civil authorities, citizens, and the state to foster the stability of family life and a culture of values that strengthen families within a society (*CCC* 2234-2246). The decisions of government officials and legislators ought to reflect God's plan for the human family, the natural law, and the dignity of each person and each family. But the family as an institution is primary, regardless of any recognition by civil authority. The family is the reference point by which different kinds of familial relationships are to be considered (*CCC* 2202).

❖ The Christian family as a "domestic Church" is the fundamental community or basic unit of the parish, diocese, and the universal Church. By fostering mutual love, respect, and forgiveness, the Christian family becomes a living and powerful witness to the Gospel as a community of faith and prayer, a school of human virtues and of love. "The future of civilization passes through the family," as it was expressed in the words of Pope John Paul II.

Read the Lesson of Faith — Bl. Maria and Bl. Luigi Quattrocchi in the *United States Catholic Catechism for Adults*, pages 373-375.

Reflection: How does the Lesson of Faith illustrate the topic of this session?

APPLICATION TO CULTURE

Discussion

The following questions may be used to guide personal/group study and reflection along with the questions provided in the *United States Catholic Catechism for Adults*, page 382:

1. Identify some challenges posed by contemporary culture to the values and dignity of the Christian family.
2. Share concrete ways in which you can strengthen your own family relationships. What challenges and obstacles do you face?
3. Name practical ways you can renew and deepen the faith life of your family, such as prayer or shared reflection on and study of Scripture.

CONCLUSION

Read the Meditation and Prayer found in the *United States Catholic Catechism for Adults*, pages 383-385.

Make participants aware of the following suggestions for further reading and study:

Pope John Paul II, On the Role of the Christian Family in the Modern World (*Familiaris Consortio*), November 22, 1981.

Second Vatican Council, Pastoral Constitution on the Church in the Modern World (*Gaudium et Spes*), 47-52.

Chapter 29
THE FIFTH COMMANDMENT: PROMOTE THE CULTURE OF LIFE

INTRODUCTION

Prayer to the Holy Spirit, page 6

Choose one of the following Scripture readings:
- Ps. 8
- Gen. 1-2
- Ex. 23:7

Reflection Time

> **The *Catechism of the Catholic Church* and the Compendium**
>
> *CCC*: 2258-2330
> Compendium:
> Questions 466-486

CATECHESIS

Read this Summary:

The Catholic Church defends the sanctity of human life as a gift from God. Human life is sacred because it originates in God's creative love. God alone is the Creator of Life from its beginning to its end; to claim the right to destroy human life is to contradict the sacred origin and nature of all human life.

The Church defends the sanctity of human life by her efforts to create and support a "culture of life." Each one of us takes our part in this "culture of life" by affirming the inviolable dignity and sacredness of life. In this way we obey the Fifth Commandment, "You shall not kill."

The Fifth Commandment forbids murder, abortion, euthanasia and physician-assisted suicide, terrorism, violence, and unjust wars that, in one way or another, threaten life. In defending the "culture of life," we invite others to recognize that the exercise of human freedom is for, not against, God's intent and plan. We also invite others to form their consciences in light of God's commands, not society's fads and values. The weakening of a Christian conscience contributes to the diminishing value placed on every human life.

❖ God's creative act is the source of the sacred value of every human life. Every human person created by God exists in relationship with God; God alone is the Lord of human life from the moment of conception to natural death.

❖ The deliberate murder of an innocent person gravely contradicts the dignity of life, the golden rule, and the sacred and creative act of God (*CCC* 2261).

❖ Direct abortion as the intended destruction of an unborn child is an act contrary to God's law and the sanctity and dignity of the most vulnerable member of the human family — a child in the womb. Because the embryo is considered a person from conception, it has a "right to life" and must be defended, cared for, and healed like any other human being (*CCC* 2322, 2323).

❖ Direct euthanasia is putting to death the sick, disabled, or the dying. Physician-assisted suicide is performed with the aid of a doctor; but suicide is morally wrong, whether committed alone or with assistance.

❖ Injustice, excessive economic or social inequalities, envy, distrust, and pride among nations continually threaten peace and cause wars. While all possible means must be taken to avoid war, there are times when legitimate defense of one's country by military force may be taken under the strictest conditions. These are known as the "Just War" conditions (*CCC* 2309).

❖ The Fifth Commandment also covers other offenses such as bigotry and hatred, physical or emotional abuse, violence of any kind against another person, inattention to one's health, or substance abuse (*CCC* 2288-2291).

Read the Lesson of Faith — Dorothy Day in the *United States Catholic Catechism for Adults*, pages 387-389.

Reflection: How does the Lesson of Faith illustrate the topic of this session?

APPLICATION TO CULTURE

Discussion

The following questions may be used to guide personal/group study and reflection along with the questions provided in the *United States Catholic Catechism for Adults*, page 400:

1. Why does the Catholic Church continue to defend the dignity and sanctity of every human life? Why is this countercultural witness important today?
2. Identify some of the root causes of the "culture of death." List concrete ways you promote the "culture of life" and the value of human life at every stage.
3. Discuss the root causes of terrorism and violence today. What are some practical ways in which Catholics foster peace and justice in society?

CONCLUSION

Read the Meditation and Prayer found in the *United States Catholic Catechism for Adults*, pages 401-402.

Make participants aware of the following suggestions for further reading and study:

Dorothy Day, *The Long Loneliness*. HarperSanFrancisco, 1997.

Pope John Paul II, On the Value and Inviolability of Human Life — the Gospel of Life (*Evangelium Vitae*), 1995.

Congregation for the Doctrine of the Faith, *Instruction on Respect for Human Life in its Origin and on the Dignity of Procreation*, 1987.

Second Vatican Council, Pastoral Constitution on the Church in the Modern World (*Gaudium et Spes*), 27.

Chapter 30

THE SIXTH COMMANDMENT: MARITAL FIDELITY

INTRODUCTION
Prayer to the Holy Spirit, page 6

Choose one of the following Scripture readings:
- Ps. 51
- Prov. 6:20-32
- Sir. 26:1-18
- Jn. 2:1-11

Reflection Time

CATECHESIS
Read this Summary:

> The **Catechism of the Catholic Church** and the **Compendium**
>
> *CCC*: 2331-2400
> Compendium:
> Questions 487-502

The Sixth Commandment calls spouses to permanent and exclusive fidelity to one another, a counter-cultural value in contemporary society. Fidelity in marriage flows from the sacramental graces of the covenant of marriage. As spouses vow to be faithful to one another forever, their words are a powerful image and witness to the covenant God made with humanity. Adultery undermines the dignity and purpose of Christian marriage and weakens individuals and the institution of the family.

Sexuality is a gift of God by which we are to participate in God's plan for men and women made in the image and likeness of God. Chastity as self-mastery and the healthy integration of sexual identity are part of God's plan for every person.

❖ The union of spouses achieves the twofold end of marriage — the good of the spouses and the transmission of life (*CCC* 2363).

❖ The sacramental bond of husband and wife is *both* unitive and procreative. The unitive aspect of marriage unites couples in marital acts of self-gift. The procreative aspect of marriage calls couples to be open to children — a gift from God, not a right (*CCC* 2378). God established an inseparable bond between the unitive and procreative aspects of marriage. Since it separates the act of conception from sexual union, artificial contraception is contrary to God's will for marriage. *In vitro* fertilization separates conception from the sexual act and is, therefore, also morally wrong.

❖ In keeping with the defense of the sanctity of life, the Catholic Church teaches that "every marriage act remain ordered *per se* to the procreation of human life" (*CCC* 2366).

❖ Chastity is the successful integration of sexuality within the person and the gradual integration of the human person in their bodily and spiritual being (*CCC* 2337).

❖ Chastity is a moral virtue. It is also a gift from God, a grace, and the fruit of spiritual effort. The Holy Spirit given in the sacraments enables one whom the water of Baptism has regenerated to imitate the purity of Christ (*CCC* 2345).

❖ Chastity as self-mastery is for all people, married, single, religious, and ordained. Chastity blossoms in friendship and respect of the dignity of each human person.

Read the Lesson of Faith — Pope Paul VI in the *United States Catholic Catechism for Adults*, pages 403-404.

Reflection: How does the Lesson of Faith illustrate the topic of this session?

APPLICATION TO CULTURE

Discussion

The following questions may be used to guide personal/group study and reflection along with the questions provided in the *United States Catholic Catechism for Adults*, page 414:

1. List challenges to the virtue of chastity today. How does your understanding of the Church's teachings on marital fidelity and chastity help you to appreciate and to grow in the virtue of chastity?

2. How can you witness to the gift of chastity in your state of life?

3. Discuss the link between the dignity of human life and the Church's teachings on marital fidelity and chastity.

4. How would you explain Catholic belief in the sanctity of marriage, and fidelity in marriage, in contrast to popular cultural approaches to marriage today?

5. How do you personally witness to chastity or marital fidelity, depending on your state of life?

CONCLUSION

Read the Meditation and Prayer found in the *United States Catholic Catechism for Adults*, pages 415-416.

Make participants aware of the following suggestions for further reading and study:

Pope Paul VI, On Human Life (*Humanae Vitae*), 1968.

Pope John Paul II, The Gospel of Life (*Evangelium Vitae*), 1995.

Second Vatican Council, Pastoral Constitution on the Church in the Modern World (*Gaudium et Spes*), 47-52.

Chapter 31

THE SEVENTH COMMANDMENT: DO NOT STEAL; ACT JUSTLY

INTRODUCTION
Prayer to the Holy Spirit, page 6

Choose one of the following Scripture readings:
- Is. 58:5-11
- Ex. 20:15
- Deut. 5:19
- Amos 5:24
- Mt. 25:34-46
- 1 Cor. 6:10

Reflection Time

> **The *Catechism of the Catholic Church* and the Compendium**
>
> *CCC*: 2401-2463
> Compendium:
> Questions 503-520

CATECHESIS
Read this Summary:

The Seventh Commandment prohibits theft — the taking of another's goods against the reasonable will of the owner. Every form of theft is contrary to God's will and constitutes an injustice against others. The injustice of theft requires recompense and restitution of stolen goods (*CCC* 2453-2454).

The rich body of Catholic social teaching touches on participation in social life, the role of civil authorities, the importance of common good, natural law, human solidarity, and a preferential love for the poor (*CCC* 1897-1948).

Major themes of Catholic social teaching that flow from the Seventh Commandment include the sanctity of human life; right to religious freedom; call to community; options for the poor and vulnerable; dignity of work and rights of workers; solidarity with the marginalized; and care for the environment.

❖ Man is the author, center, and goal of all economic and social life. All of God's creation, meant for everyone, should in fact reach everyone in accordance with justice and charity (*CCC* 2402-2406, 2459).

❖ The Church makes a judgment about social, economic, and political matters when the basic rights of every human being require it. The Catholic Church sees fit to teach on these social issues because the temporal and common welfare of every human being is ordered to their final end, who is God (*CCC* 2458). In order to better understand and explain the Catholic Church's response to social, economic, and political challenges, Catholics are invited to discuss and reflect on the tradition of papal, conciliar, and episcopal conference documents.

❖ The major themes taken up in Catholic social teaching include the dignity and sanctity of human life, the need for community, the option for the poor, the right to religious freedom, the rights of workers and the dignity of work, and the care for the environment (*CCC* 2419-2442).

❖ The key issue in Catholic social teaching is justice for all, especially for the poor and the vulnerable. The Church commits her efforts to the removal of the symptoms and root causes of poverty and injustice.

❖ Love for the poor is a priority for every disciple of Christ, who looked with great care and compassion on the poor. Giving alms to the poor is a witness to love and a work of justice pleasing to God (*CCC* 2462).

❖ God granted man dominion over creation, and the exercise of just and careful stewardship over creation flows from the Seventh Commandment.

Read the Lesson of Faith — Mother Joseph in the *United States Catholic Catechism for Adults*, pages 417-418.

Reflection: How does the Lesson of Faith illustrate the topic of this session?

APPLICATION TO CULTURE

Discussion

The following questions may be used to guide personal/group study and reflection along with the questions provided in the *United States Catholic Catechism for Adults,* page 425:

1. How do you apply the Seventh Commandment in the daily circumstances of your life?
2. The Catholic Church has developed a rich body of social teachings. Why is it that the Church sees fit to teach on social, economic, and political matters?
3. Which of the many social justice issues touches your life personally in one way or another? How are you concretely called to participate in the Church's commitment to create a just world?

CONCLUSION

Read the Meditation and Prayer found in the *United States Catholic Catechism for Adults,* pages 427-428.

Make participants aware of the following suggestions for further reading and study:

Pope John Paul II, On the Dignity of Work (*Laborem Exercens*), 1981.

————, On Social Justice (*Solicitudo rei socialis*), 1987.

————, *Centesimus Annus*, 1991.

Pontifical Council for Justice and Peace, *Compendium of the Social Doctrine of the Church,* 2004.

Chapter 32

THE EIGHTH COMMANDMENT: TELL THE TRUTH

INTRODUCTION
Prayer to the Holy Spirit, page 6

Choose one of the following Scripture readings:
- Ps. 26
- Ex. 20:16
- Mt. 5:33-37
- Jn. 1:14; 8:12; 12:46; 14:16;
- Rom. 3:4
- 1 Pet. 3:15-16

Reflection Time

CATECHESIS
Read this Summary:

God is the source of all truth. Christ Jesus not only taught truth, he spoke of himself, saying, "I am the Truth" (Jn. 14:6) The Eighth Commandment urges the telling of truth and the avoidance of lies in all its forms.

The Scriptures give us concrete examples of offenses against truth. We break this Commandment when we ruin the reputation of another by telling lies, when we practice rash judgments against another, when we engage in detraction (the unjust telling of someone's faults), perjury (lying under oath), or calumny (lying about another).

The Christian tradition also gives us countless examples of men and women who upheld the truth to the point of death. We witness to the truth that comes from God in our daily lives when we proclaim the Gospel in word and in deed. When we speak the truth in love, we invite others to understand and live in the freedom of the truth.

Art gives sensory form to the truth of human existence. Christian art gives sensory form to the truths of revelation that we hold in faith. Truth, beauty, and goodness reflect the nature of God, and through them, we participate in the life of God.

> **The *Catechism of the Catholic Church* and the Compendium**
>
> *CCC*: 2464-2513
> Compendium:
> Questions 521-526

❖ "You shall not bear false witness against your neighbor" (Ex. 20:16). To live in the truth and to speak the truth is to live in God who is the source of all truth. Jesus spoke of himself, saying, "I am the Truth" (Jn. 14:16).

❖ Truth or truthfulness is the virtue by which we show ourselves to be true in word and in deed. As disciples of Christ, we strive to "live in the truth" that is in the simplicity of a life lived in conformity with Jesus' own example (*CCC* 2468-2470).

❖ All Christians are called to witness to the Gospel truth of the saving life, death, and resurrection of Jesus Christ. This witness takes place in words and in our deeds. Martyrdom is the supreme witness given to the truth of faith. Even in our own times, Christians throughout the world continue to give their lives for the truth of the Gospel (*CCC* 2471-2472).

❖ Offenses against truth include false witness and perjury, rash judgment and detraction, and calumny that destroys another's reputation. Flattery and boasting also offend against the truth of reality (*CCC* 2475-2487).

❖ Offenses against truth require reparation, particularly when a person's good name has been destroyed (*CCC* 2509).

❖ Members of the media and those involved in mass communication have the responsibility to put their work at the service of the truth for the common good. Society has a right to information from the media based on truth, justice, and freedom (*CCC* 2493-2499).

❖ The fine arts express in sensory forms the truth of God, the created world, and the human person. Sacred art is true and beautiful when its form corresponds to its vocation: "evoking and glorifying, in faith and adoration, the transcendent mystery of God — the surpassing invisible beauty of truth and love visible in Christ, who reflects the glory of God and bears the very stamp of his nature." Genuine sacred art draws us to adoration, to prayer, and to love of God (*CCC* 2500-2503).

Read the Lesson of Faith — Bishop John Francis Noll in the *United States Catholic Catechism for Adults*, pages 429-430.

Reflection: How does the Lesson of Faith illustrate the topic of this session?

APPLICATION TO CULTURE

Discussion

The following questions may be used to guide personal/group study and reflection along with the questions provided in the *United States Catholic Catechism for Adults,* page 436:

1. How do you live by the Eighth Commandment in daily life situations — at work, at home, in your faith community and neighborhood?
2. Where do you observe offenses against truth in everyday life and popular culture?
3. How does religious and sacred art reflect the infinite truth and beauty of God?

CONCLUSION

Read the Meditation and Prayer found in the *United States Catholic Catechism for Adults,* pages 437-438.

Make participants aware of the following suggestions for further reading and study:

Ann Ball with Fr. Leon Hutton, *Champion of the Church: The Extraordinary Life and Legacy of Archbishop Noll.* Our Sunday Visitor, 2006.

Second Vatican Council, Decree on the Media of Social Communications (*Inter Mirifica*), 1963.

Pope John Paul II, *Letter to Artists,* 1999.

Chapter 33

THE NINTH COMMANDMENT: PRACTICE PURITY OF HEART

INTRODUCTION

Prayer to the Holy Spirit, page 6

Choose one of the following Scripture readings:
- Ps. 121
- Mt. 5:8; 15:19
- 1 Cor. 13:12
- 1 Jn. 3:2

Reflection Time

The *Catechism of the Catholic Church* and the Compendium

CCC: 2514-2533
Compendium:
Questions 527-530

CATECHESIS

Read this Summary:

The Ninth Commandment teaches us to guard ourselves against impurity of heart. The heart is the seat of moral acts, and the grace of the sacraments strengthens and preserves us from impurities of heart, mind, and body. In the midst of a society that glorifies immodesty, indecency, and sexual permissiveness, the Ninth Commandment challenges Christians. Through the practice of purity of heart, we become a countercultural sign.

To be human is to experience the struggle between spiritual and physical desires, a struggle that is the effect of Original Sin. The grace of Baptism purifies us from sin, but the tendency or inclination to sin, also called *concupiscence,* remains.

Purification of the heart comes through the discipline of prayer and study of God's word. Modesty, a virtue of the Christian life, is necessary for purity. Modesty protects the dignity and mystery of the person and guards against exploitation of one by another. Modesty builds purity of heart, a gift through which we live out God's plan for our personal relationships, human sexuality, and marriage.

❖ The Ninth Commandment warns against lust or carnal concupiscence. "You shall not covet your neighbor's wife" (Deut. 5:21) and "everyone who looks at a woman lustfully has already committed adultery with her in his heart" (Mt. 5:28) (*CCC* 2528-2529).

❖ Concupiscence refers to the disordered desires and the inclination to sin that is the result of Original Sin. It also describes the state of humanity in rebellion of the passions and desires against God (*CCC* 405, 2515).

❖ Because human beings are made up of spirit and body, there exists a certain tension, a struggle between the tendencies of the "spirit" and that of the "flesh." This struggle is part of the experience of spiritual battle (*CCC* 2516).

❖ "Blessed are the pure in heart, for they shall see God" is the sixth beatitude. This purity of heart is a precondition for the vision of God, and even now it enables us to see as God sees, to see our bodies as a temple of the Holy Spirit and to see the image of God in our neighbor (*CCC* 2517-2519).

❖ Modesty protects the inner spiritual mystery of the human person and protects love. It encourages patience and moderation in loving relationships. A modest person dresses, speaks and acts in a way that supports and encourages purity and chastity rather than in a way that tempts lust and sinful acts (*CCC* 2521-2524).

❖ We purify our hearts and minds by perseverance in prayer, the grace of the sacraments and the Word of God, the practice of chastity, and modesty (*CCC* 2520).

Read the Lesson of Faith — St. Maria Goretti in the *United States Catholic Catechism for Adults*, pages 439-440.

Reflection: How does the Lesson of Faith illustrate the topic of this session?

APPLICATION TO CULTURE

Discussion

The following questions may be used to guide personal/group study and reflection along with the questions provided in the *United States Catholic Catechism for Adults,* page 444:

1. How would you explain Catholic teachings on modesty and purity of heart to a young person? (*CCC* 1832, 2521-2524)
2. How might Christians help to reverse society's values and messages that undermine modesty and purity of heart?
3. Discuss the example of one American saint or someone you know personally who witnesses to the virtue of modesty.

CONCLUSION

Read the Meditation and Prayer found in the *United States Catholic Catechism for Adults,* pages 445-446.

Make participants aware of the following suggestions for further reading and study:
   Pope John Paul II, *Original Unity of Man and Woman,* Wednesday Catechesis.
   Second Vatican Council, Pastoral Constitution on the Church in the Modern World (*Gaudium et Spes*), 58.
   St. Augustine, *Confessions.*

Chapter 34 &

THE TENTH COMMANDMENT:
EMBRACE POVERTY OF SPIRIT

INTRODUCTION
Prayer to the Holy Spirit, page 6

Choose one of the following Scripture readings:
- Ps. 49
- Mt. 6:19-21
- Mk. 8:35
- Lk. 14:33
- 1 Tim. 6:10
- Gal. 5:24

Reflection Time

> **The *Catechism of the Catholic Church* and the Compendium**
>
> *CCC:* 2534-2557
> Compendium:
> Questions 531-533

CATECHESIS
Read this Summary:

The Tenth Commandment extends the meaning of the Seventh and Ninth Commandments as it urges poverty of spirit and generosity of heart. These virtues free us from envy, greed, and excessive materialism. This Commandment is yet another means by which Christians living in the midst of a consumerist and materialistic society become a countercultural witness in their imitation of Christ Jesus.

In the first of the Beatitudes, Jesus speaks of poverty of spirit as the way to inherit the Kingdom of God. To grow in poverty of spirit requires detachment from material goods and wealth. Our desire should be for spiritual riches that are freely and abundantly given by God.

Greed and envy as companion vices are obstacles to growth in poverty of spirit. Envy leads us to covet another's goods, wealth, and fame. Greed is the distortion of the desire for wealth, stability, and prosperity. Poverty of spirit strengthens us to overcome envy and greed and trust in God's provident care for our every need.

Christian stewardship invites us to receive God's gifts from creation and the material world, to cultivate them responsibly and justly, and share them with others, especially with those in need. To be a disciple of Christ calls us to be faithful and generous stewards of the created order, our vocation, and the Church.

❖ The Tenth Commandment forbids the coveting of goods of another, as well as the desire to amass earthly goods without limit. It requires that the sin of envy be uprooted from the heart, as greed and envy prevent us from growing in poverty of spirit. Thus, it concerns the intentions of the heart and summarizes all the precepts of the Law (*CCC* 2534).

❖ Throughout the Gospels, Jesus teaches his disciples detachment from earthly possessions. He reminds them that "where your treasure is, there will your heart be also" (Mt. 6:21). Trust in God's provident care replaces the anxieties that come with greed and envy (*CCC* 2544-2547).

❖ Growing in our desire for true happiness that comes from God frees us from excessive attachment to material wealth and possessions (*CCC* 2548-2550).

Read the Lesson of Faith — Mother Henriette Delille in the *United States Catholic Catechism for Adults*, pages 447-448.

Reflection: How does the Lesson of Faith illustrate the topic of this session?

APPLICATION TO CULTURE

Discussion

The following questions may be used to guide personal/group study and reflection along with the questions provided in the *United States Catholic Catechism for Adults*, page 455:

1. Discuss how envy and greed are daily reinforced in our culture through the media.
2. How can you grow in detachment from worldly goods in imitation of Jesus? How can you deepen a spirit of generosity to others, especially the poor?
3. How do you exercise Christian stewardship over the created world, your vocation and state in life, and toward the Church?

CONCLUSION

Read the Meditation and Prayer found in the *United States Catholic Catechism for Adults*, pages 456-457.

Make participants aware of the following suggestions for further reading and study:

Cyprian Davis, OSB, *Henriette Delille: Servant of Slaves, Witness to the Poor*. Sisters of the Holy Family, 1999.

United States Conference of Catholic Bishops, *Stewardship: A Disciple's Response* (A Pastoral Letter on Stewardship), 2002.

Chapter 35

GOD CALLS US TO PRAY: THE FOUNDATIONS OF PRAYER

INTRODUCTION

Prayer to the Holy Spirit, page 6

Choose one of the following Scripture readings:
- Ps. 130
- Ex. 33:11
- 1 Sam. 3:9-10
- 1 Thess. 5:17
- Rom. 8:26

Reflection Time

The *Catechism of the Catholic Church* and the Compendium

CCC: 2558-2758
Compendium:
Questions 534-577

CATECHESIS

Read this Summary:

Prayer stands at the heart of our relationship with God. In prayer, a believer humbly seeks to grow in union with God, revealed in Jesus Christ, in the power of the Holy Spirit. Prayer is a response of faith to God and reveals a divine-human dialogue of love, forgiveness, mercy, and grace.

Jesus taught his disciples to pray with humble and faithful hearts and minds. He encouraged them to watchfulness and boldness in prayer as they offered themselves and their petitions to God.

The Church, born in prayer, lives and grows in prayer as well. The Holy Spirit inspires the faithful in every age of the Church to a life of prayer. The basic forms of Christian prayer are adoration, petition, repentance, intercession, thanksgiving, and praise (*CCC* 2623-2649); the three kinds of prayer are vocal, meditative, and contemplative. Christian prayer is always Trinitarian in that we pray in the name of the Father, and of the Son, and the Holy Spirit. Daily prayer helps to strengthen us to live in the midst of the world with its joys and anxieties, its successes and challenges. Prayer and Christian living are inseparable. The Word of God, the Eucharist, daily personal prayer, the Liturgy of the Hours, and the feasts of the Liturgical Year are all invitations to Christian prayer (*CCC* 2700-2724).

❖ "Prayer is the raising of one's mind and heart to God." It is our response in faith to God's loving plan of salvation and the divine desire for communion with us (*CCC* 2561).

❖ Throughout the Bible, prayer is a dialogue between God and humanity. God constantly seeks us out. Our restless hearts, distracted by sin, blind us to God's desire for communion with us. Prayer is the point of intersection between God's call and our desire and response to grace (*CCC* 2568-2589).

❖ Jesus taught his disciples to pray always, with faith and perseverance, and in humility and watchfulness (*CCC* 2598-2616).

❖ The Mother of God, the Virgin Mary, is an outstanding example of prayer. In her *Fiat* and *Magnificat*, she offers her whole being to God in faith (*CCC* 2617-2622).

❖ The main obstacles to prayer are distractions and dryness. Perseverance, trust, and ongoing conversion aid us in perseverance in prayer (*CCC* 2725-2758).

❖ The family as the domestic Church is the first school of prayer, and parents are the first teachers of prayer. Saints and other Christian witnesses remind us of the necessity of prayer in Christian discipleship.

❖ The Eucharist contains and expresses all forms of prayer; it is a "pure offering" of the Body of Christ to God's name. It is *the* sacrifice of praise (*CCC* 2643).

Read the Lesson of Faith — Archbishop Fulton J. Sheen in the *United States Catholic Catechism for Adults*, pages 461-462.

Reflection: How does the Lesson of Faith illustrate the topic of this session?

APPLICATION TO CULTURE

Discussion

The following questions may be used to guide personal/group study and reflection along with the questions provided in the *United States Catholic Catechism for Adults,* page 478:

1. Describe your life of prayer. Name both positive elements and challenges or difficulties in prayer (*CCC* 2725-2758).
2. How can you renew a spirit of prayer in your home, with family members, and children?
3. What is your favorite Christian prayer? In what way could your participation in Sunday Eucharist strengthen your commitment to daily prayer?

CONCLUSION

Read the Meditation and Prayer found in the *United States Catholic Catechism for Adults,* pages 479-480.

Make participants aware of the following suggestions for further reading and study:

Fulton J. Sheen, *Treasure in Clay: The Autobiography of Fulton J. Sheen.* Image Books, 1993.

Fulton J. Sheen, Michael Dubruiel, *Praying in the Presence of Our Lord with Fulton J. Sheen.* Our Sunday Visitor, 2002.

Pope John Paul II, The Coming Third Christian Millennium (*Novo Millenio Ineunte*), 32-34.

Chapter 36

JESUS TAUGHT US TO PRAY THE LORD'S PRAYER: THE "OUR FATHER"

INTRODUCTION
Prayer to the Holy Spirit, page 6

Choose one of the following Scripture readings:
- Mt. 6:5-13
- Lk. 11:1, 9-13; 18:10-14
- Rom. 5:5

Reflection Time

The *Catechism of the Catholic Church* and the Compendium

CCC: 2759-2865
Compendium:
Questions 578-598

CATECHESIS
Read this Summary:

Jesus teaches his disciples and us to pray in the words of the "Our Father." The Lord's Prayer is the most perfect of prayers, containing all that we rightly desire before God. The "Our Father" is at the heart of every personal and communal prayer.

There are two versions of the "Our Father" in the Gospels. Luke gives us five petitions, while Matthew gives seven, The Church's liturgy prays Matthew's version. The Lord's Prayer is a summary of the entire Gospel and is a central part of Christian prayer in the Liturgy of the Hours, the sacraments of Initiation, and particularly the Eucharist.

In the "Our Father," the first three petitions are addressed to the glory of the Father, the sanctification of his Holy Name, the coming of God's Kingdom and the fulfillment of the divine will. The remaining four petitions place our human needs before God; asking that our lives be nourished, healed of sin, and made victorious in the struggle of the world.

In the final "Amen," which means "so be it," we affirm in faith our confidence and trust in God our Father, his Son Jesus Christ our Lord, and the Holy Spirit, who dwells in our midst. The "Our Father" is a gift through which we return time and time again to Jesus, who leads us to God in the power of the Holy Spirit.

Read the Lesson of Faith — Jesus teaches us how to pray, in the *United States Catholic Catechism for Adults*, pages 481-482.

Reflection: How does the Lesson of Faith illustrate the topic of this session?

APPLICATION TO CULTURE

Discussion

The following questions may be used to guide personal/group study and reflection along with the questions provided in the *United States Catholic Catechism for Adults,* page 492:

1. How would you explain the "Our Father" as a summary of the whole Gospel? (*CCC* 2774, 2776)
2. What do the first three petitions of the Lord's Prayer mean to you personally?
3. How do the last four petitions of the Lord's Prayer affect your daily living of the Gospel?

CONCLUSION

Read the Meditation and Prayer found in the *United States Catholic Catechism for Adults,* pages 494-495.

Make participants aware of the following suggestions for further reading and study:

Tertullian, *On Prayer.*

Pope John Paul II, The Coming Third Christian Millennium (*Novo Millennio Ineunte*), 32-34.

St. Augustine, *Commentaries on the Our Father.*

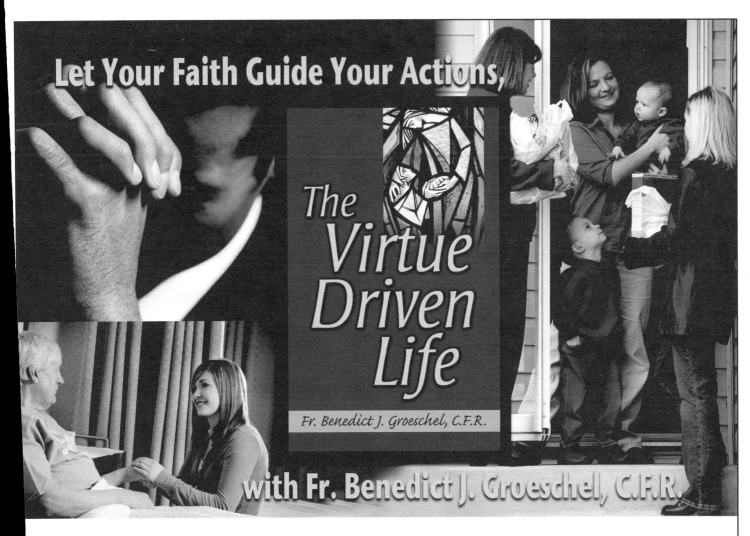

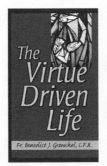